The Simple Subs Book

Other Titles of Interest

The Simple Subs Book

by
LESLIE SELLERS

SECOND EDITION

PERGAMON PRESS
OXFORD · NEW YORK · BEIJING · FRANKFURT
SÃO PAULO · SYDNEY · TOKYO · TORONTO

U.K.	Pergamon Press, Headington Hill Hall, Oxford OX3 0BW, England
U.S.A.	Pergamon Press, Maxwell House, Fairview Park, Elmsford, New York 10523, U.S.A.
PEOPLE'S REPUBLIC OF CHINA	Pergamon Press, Room 4037, Qianmen Hotel, Beijing, People's Republic of China
FEDERAL REPUBLIC OF GERMANY	Pergamon Press, Hammerweg 6, D-6242 Kronberg, Federal Republic of Germany
BRAZIL	Pergamon Editora, Rua Eça de Queiros, 346, CEP 04011, Paraiso, São Paulo, Brazil
AUSTRALIA	Pergamon Press Australia, P.O. Box 544, Potts Point, N.S.W. 2011, Australia
JAPAN	Pergamon Press, 8th Floor, Matsuoka Central Building, 1-7-1 Nishishinjuku, Shinjuku-ku, Tokyo 160, Japan
CANADA	Pergamon Press Canada, Suite No 271, 253 College Street, Toronto, Ontario, Canada M5T 1R5

Copyright © 1985 Leslie Sellers

First edition 1968
Reprinted 1969, 1979, 1982
Second edition 1985
Reprinted 1988

Library of Congress Cataloging in Publication Data
Sellers, Leslie.
The simple subs book.
(Pergamon international library of science, technology, engineering, and social studies)
Includes index.
1. Copy-reading.   I. Title.   II. Series.
PN4784.C75S44   1985   070.4'15   84–26546

British Library Cataloguing in Publication Data
Sellers, Leslie
The simple subs book.–2nd ed.–(Pergamon international library)
1. Journalism–Editing
I. Title
070.4'15   PN4778

ISBN 0-08-031839-8 (Hardcover)
ISBN 0-08-031840-1 (Flexicover)

Printed in Great Britain by A. Wheaton & Co. Ltd., Exeter

PREFACE TO THE SECOND EDITION

No one was more surprised than I at the appearance of a second printing of *The Simple Subs Book* within months of the first. And I suppose no one more surprised than me at the appearance of a second edition, 16 years on, with me looking slightly older and weightier than the picture on the back cover.

I had hoped, in my more optimistic moods, that it might sell at a steady conversion rate of three pints of bitter a week. But clearly there were more subs — or more people waiting to read about subbing — than I e'er dream'd on.

It got on the telly, and on the radio. It was reviewed in the most unlikely quarters, and even commended to the Church as The Book No Parish Magazine Editor Should Be Without.

It brought no libel writs, in spite of all the references to personalities, and practically no complaints apart from those about split infinitives, written by one of my most persistent correspondents.

It drew letters from all over the world, including one from the head of a department of languages in a French university who addressed the envelope to
> M. Leslie Sellers
> Professeur of Journalese.

Over the years, I've personally come across copies in Australia, New Zealand, South Africa, Singapore, the US, Ireland, France, Greece and Rhodesia as was. Not to mention Ceylon, where an excited young man battered a path through the flies in Columbo Airport and triumphantly brandished a copy before me. He talked so quickly I still don't know who he was.

One reviewer did complain that the book was oversexed — and this notwithstanding the fact that the editor insisted for decency's sake on altering *Altrincham Buggery Club* (which did exist) to *Altrincham Adultery Club* (which as far as I know didn't). This was more than compensated for by the favourable comments in the religious periodicals.

There was one real protest, about my defence of the cliché *kiss of life*. It made such a good point that I gave it a lot of thought:

As an ex-member of the St John Ambulance Brigade, I strongly dislike the "kiss of life" gag. A kiss is a SUCKING effort, whereas what is essential is a BLOWING one. This must be kept in the mind of the first-aider all the time. The "breath of life" would have been a better cliché. Sorry to contradict you, but "kiss of life" does NOT express "precisely what is meant"; except to the low-minded bystander, useless and obstructive, who doesn't know what is going on. One is blowing up paper bags, not kissing the aperture. So hats off to Mr Edwin Gay.

Hell, I thought — if we start talking about *breath of life*, who'll know *what* we're talking about?

And that's the important thing about newspapers: People have got to know what you're talking about.

LESLIE SELLERS

CONTENTS

Stop worrying about Kemsley – he's dead

I SOMETIMES get the impression that it's obligatory for every book on journalism to begin with an historical dissertation, preferably one mentioning W T Stead, John Walter, *The Daily Universal Register,* Jeremiah Garnett, Lord Kemsley, Johann Gutenberg, and what The Chief said to somebody in 1909.

This book is going to be an exception. Sub-editors, let's face it, haven't any history to speak of. Their arrival on the scene is due to two factors — the size and complexity of modern newspaper organisations, and the increasing concentration on both readability and design.

There wasn't much need for subs in the days when dispatches "From our own correspondent, Balaclava, Wednesday, delayed" were sent to the Printer to be set all 7 point solid and then just run in as far as they'd go.

Likewise, a main news page top with the headline

THE ASHANTIS

NEWS FROM KUMASI

indicates that such subs as were around then bore little resemblance to those at large today.

Indeed, the whole concept of the sub-editor's work has changed so vastly in its short history that the historical background is largely irrelevant. We all *know* what Lord Northcliffe did for the newspaper industry in 1906, and are duly grateful. It was he who started the whole process off. But of more immediate concern to the sub-editor is what *The Mirror* did with its centre spread yesterday, and what conceivable new angle/heading the *Sun* will find for its latest sex series tomorrow.

Sub-editors now are in a position of considerable power in any newspaper office. They have a prime influence on the style, crispness and newsiness of the paper. In the heyday of Arthur Christiansen, when the *Daily Express* was known (either enviously or sneeringly) as the subs' paper, they used it to make the whole production seem as though it were written by one man, and we all know who the one man was.

It is in the big, highly-tuned newspapers that the craft of subbing is developed to the highest degree. When it is possible to employ a big staff, the work-load on the individual becomes less and more time can be spent on the kind of polish that distinguishes the best-selling national newspapers. And the sub *is* in the polishing business.

Most of the real lessons in subbing are to be learned from the popular dailies. The "heavies", although they insist on a rigid adherence to house style (and that's good training for any sub), tend to lean much more heavily on experienced staff writers, often running them at great length. They also keep to fairly stereotyped settings and design.

With the popular papers, where the actual selling of a story assumes far greater importance, the sub comes much more into his own.

On any big subs' table there are vast diversities of background and temperament, and this is all to the good. A table consisting entirely of geniuses would be a disaster.

Men who are quite incapable of writing a happy, laughing centre column, or turning 30 sheets of an agency court report into a tear-jerker of a home page lead, are frequently enormously valuable subs because of other talents. They are often the men who are utterly reliable when it comes to cutting a specialist's story by half, who sub to exact length, who never bust headings, who can be trusted absolutely to put through a complex page exactly as visualised. Every office needs them.

Similarly, the sub who writes the sparkling caption or the gay spring-in-the-air story, and is invaluable for that reason, may well make the most disastrous errors of judgement on length, be totally unable to write a heading that fits, and make off in the direction of a nervous breakdown if he's given a running story about an air crash.

These differences in temperament and make-up can be borne in big offices, and if properly utilised and channelled will improve the quality of the newspaper. A touch of genius in one direction is enough. But in newspapers with few subs the all-rounder is vital, and it is with the all-round qualities that this book is concerned.

C'est magnifique, mais ce n'est pas le subbing

LET us first establish what subbing is about — and, equally important, what it's not about, for some subs have strange ideas about what they're there for. A sub is required to do five basic things:

1. To process any story he is given to the length and style laid down by his executives.

2. To mark the copy with setting instructions so clearly and carefully that there is no possibility of a come-back from the Printer or anybody else.*

3. To ensure that everything checkable has been checked — and that goes for names, places, titles, dates and anything else that could possibly be wrong.

4. To write a headline that fits, unless one has already been provided by some executive who thinks he can do it better.

5. To make sure that the story as subbed is intelligible, easy to read, and appetising.

It is at the fifth hurdle that many young sub-editors, and some old ones who ought to know better, fall flat on their faces. Let me say right away, in letters of bold, and bold caps at that, **IT IS NO PART OF A SUB'S JOB TO REWRITE A STORY THAT DOESN'T NEED REWRITING.**

That is an elementary rule of subbing. If a story is already intelligible, appetising, and easy to read, that is enough. But there are still itchy-fingered subs around who rewrite everything at the drop of a paper-clip, and sometimes end up with a story inferior to that they started with. There are good reasons why *unnecessary* rewriting if frowned upon:

IT IS BAD because it is time-wasting, and in a newspaper office time is the most important single factor. There are too many stories that do need a lot of attention to mess about with stories that don't.

---

*Certain things in this chapter (and other parts of the book) assume that subs ARE still sending copy to the Printer, though of course in many places they're typesetting themselves electronically with all the advantages that ensue. This is covered in a new chapter, Electronic Editing.

IT IS BAD because it is damaging to morale for a reporter to know that his story will always be rewritten, whether it's good or bad. This way there is no encouragement to do a decent, tidy job.

IT IS BAD because it increases the tendency to error. "Aged 56" can become "aged 65", and "Davison" become "Davidson" — and that sort of thing doesn't happen with subbing on original copy.

It's never "just ticking"

Subbing means rewriting *at times,* and the times need to be chosen with care. They occur when a story is badly done, and needs recasting completely; when two or three stories need blending into one coherent whole; when a story is so outrageously overwritten as to be impossible to deal with on raw copy; or when a reporter has tried over-hard on a gimmick approach and just failed to come off.

Many subs bristle when they are given what they dismiss contemptuously as "ticking jobs" or "par-markers". It offends their creative instincts. This is understandable, because the good sub prefers the big, off-routine job. But even the par-marking operation contains its own challenges.

It can be done with speed, thereby helping along with production of the newspaper on the day all copy is late which is most days.

It can have all errors of fact and style eliminated.

It can be the one story in the page which appears at the exact length required, because it's easier to cast off on a straight slab of typescript.

It can have a heading which is even better than the story, and presumably that was pretty good or the chief sub wouldn't have asked for it par-marked.

It can have cross-heads which have some virtues other than purely optical ones, perhaps nothing more than the theme idea to catch the reader's eye:

Happy Harold	**The kissing**
Gruntled George	**The killing**

MORAL: Even on a ticking job there's more than ticking to do.

A sub's task, then, is not to rewrite everything that lands in his hot and sticky hands. It is not even to make a mark on every folio of copy, just to show that he's read it. Put it the broadest sense it is this:

TO APPROACH EVERY STORY FROM THE POINT OF VIEW OF THE READER.

Old Coué used to urge people to cure themselves of disease by saying every morning: "Day by day and in every way I am getting better and better."

4

Old Sellers urges subs to prevent themselves becoming ingrowing and out of touch by saying every evening: "Day by day, night by night, I must never lose sight of the man who's reading the paper."

The sub is the last line of defence between the reader and the newspaper. It is he who, in the final analysis, has got to knock the story into the kind of shape that will make the customer not only start reading it but carry on till the end.

The customer, that's you

His news sense must be reader's news sense, professionally sharpened. He has to be able to pick out the dominant fact, or the talking point, and put it right there at the top so that there is no danger of the customer missing it. In a sense he is doing the customer's work for him, in the same way as the man who sells prepared or predigested food. People eat more peas now because Charlie Birdseye found a way to quick-freeze them and so made it easy. People read more newspapers now because men like Northcliffe and Beaverbrook and Bartholomew, to name but the dead, found a way to quick-thaw news and so widen the market.

This news sense has to exist and be sharpened not in a vacuum but in relation to the particular newspaper handing out the brass on Friday or the last day of the month. News is not an abstraction. It can only be considered in the context of the newspaper and its market. This can best be demonstrated geographically.

A house blows up in Glossop, and a child's corpse is found in the rubble. The treatment runs:

A big splash in the *Glossop Chronicle*. Be sure the locals will lap up every detail.

A top, quite likely on Page One, in the *Manchester Evening News*. It's the only evening paper covering Glossop, but they've got other places to think of.

A short, in the page or on the overmatter, in the London edition of the *Daily Mail*. Who in Surbiton cares a great deal about a dead child in Glossop?

Nothing at all in *Svenska Dagbladet* (Stockholm edition) or, come to that, in *Der Tagesspiegel* (Berlin) either.

But suppose the situation had been reversed, and Stockholm had been agog with the thought of someone dying other than by natural causes or suicide? Then presumably *Svenska Dagbladet* would have carried a thorough account of the sad happening. In England it might have been sent out as an optional short for the foreign page. In Manchester it could have got in an early edition as a filler. But the *Glossop Chronicle,* convinced (and rightly from their point of view) that civilisation ends at Broadbottom, would have ignored it completely.

This news-in-context principle applies not only geographically. It applies also to the readership of a newspaper, and the kind of market that it is aiming at. The stockbroker travelling to town on the 9.30 from Virginia Water is a different kind of animal to the builder's labourer travelling to Peckham Rye on the 7.52 from St Mary Cray. The two are not only interested in different subjects, but their mental approach to news is different. They represent *The Times* on the one hand, and the *Sun* on the other.

Of course there are overlaps, and stockbrokers buy the *Sun* and bricklayers buy *The Times*. But newspapers recognise that the central core of their readership is of a particular kind, and however vague and ill-defined the circulation may become at the edges it is important never to lose sight of the basic market.

The sub needs always to have a consciousness of the kind of market he is aiming at. It is no conceivable use a man joining *The Guardian* and expecting to be constantly subbing stories about mystery sex maniacs with staring eyes striking fear into the hearts of Wandsworth wives, or working for the *Daily Star* and pining because he's not asked to write captions on pictures of sunsets on Dartmoor. It should be self-evident that this is not what these newspapers are about.

But what is equally true is that the approach to stories on the part of the sub must also be conditioned by the kind of newspaper he is working for.

The news that a pop star has been nicked for a drugs offence gets the adrenalin moving both with the stockbroker from Virginia Water and the bricklayer from St Mary Cray. The story gets the big deal in both the heavies and the populars, but in a different kind of way.

In the heavies it will have the length but not the breadth. The story will be treated with dignity. (In *The Times* the pop star will be called "Mr".) Any element of approval or disapproval will be kept for the leading article. But in the popular papers display will run riot and the text will generate a great deal of excitement, varying in degree according to which end of the popular spectrum the newspaper is on.

Again, a complex speech on the Common Market by the French President will be spelt out splendidly by *The Mirror,* so that even the dimmest can understand what he was on about. But *The Times*, while translating it from the French, will tend to assume a certain amount of knowledge on the part of its readers.

The sub's approach to the treatment of the news must therefore be conditioned by the newspaper he is working for, and this applies equally to the selection of the news. A new Home Secretary in Malaysia (if they have such a thing there) will surely have his appointment recorded in *The Times*, but it is quite likely that the poor chap will end on the Page Two overmatter with the *Daily Mail*.

One hint that the Altrincham Buggery Club had been revived and one Sunday newspaper will have a reporter on the next train north to investigate, but another will probably ignore the matter completely lest its great Puritan founder should find some way of contacting the newspaper from wherever he is at the moment.

The moral of all that is that the sub must read and absorb the newspaper he is working for, so that he can (in the words of the Act) provide goods of the nature and substance demanded. These goods are those that the specific market of the newspaper — that is the reader — demands.

Sub-editors-atten-SHUN!

Newspapermen generally, and Fleet Street men in particular, sometimes appear to outsiders to be a disorganised, self-willed, wayward rabble. This is the gravest misconception.

The most successful newspapers are in fact highly-disciplined organisations. The reason for this is simple. The successful newspapers have a clearly-defined chain of command, and a firm policy and purpose which the staff must accept or go elsewhere. I remember Christiansen saying sharply, when he heard a chapel official describing his colleagues as wage-slaves: "If anyone here regards himself as a slave I am prepared to set him free at once."

The sub-editor is not a slave. He is free to exercise influence on his newspaper subject to the overall policy laid down, or if he disagrees profoundly with that policy to seek employment on a newspaper that he finds more congenial. The only freedom denied to him is to consistently and deliberately sabotage his newspaper from within.

This "freedom" would be the negation of all professionalism. It would make no more sense than it would have done to have an aeroplane designer spending all his working hours trying to indoctrinate his colleagues with the idea that it would only get off the ground if the length of the fuselage were doubled and the wing-span cut by half. A newspaper *has* to get off the ground every publication day, and on time.

Therefore it is essential for the sub-editor, whatever his temperament, to accept the existence of a chain of command — and one that doesn't only affect him. The night editor may well disagree with the editor's choice of a Page One picture. He is then entitled to put his own view, and either convince the editor of the error of his ways or, if that fails, retire gracefully. Similarly, the sub is entitled to point out the flaws in a page lead, which makes it unworthy of the position, or to suggest that it is worth twice as much space, or only half as much. But if his representations fail, perhaps for perfectly valid reasons of which he knows nothing,* his only course then is to get on with subbing the story.

The golden rule with subbing, as with so many other things, is this: **IF YOU'VE GOT ANYTHING TO SAY — SPEAK UP. THEN BELT UP.**

The only one absolutely intolerable thing in an organisation like a newspaper is to go on arguing all night, or all week as the case may be. No successful newspaper can operate, to use the words of Mr Alan Jenkins when he was night editor of the *Daily Mail,* on the basis of everybody talking and nobody listening.

This acceptance of the newspaper's attitudes involves another aspect, and that is a clear day-by-day understanding of what it is doing. That means that the sub must read, with reasonable care, each issue of his own newspaper. The most damning sentence that can be uttered about any sub, and I've heard it said so often by one executive to another, is: "*Doesn't he read the bloody paper?*" It usually comes when a sub has angled a story on the same line that appeared in column seven of page eleven the previous day, perhaps only in the last edition; or when he's written a headline on yesterday's news. Whatever the cause, it has an element of damnation in it.

No sub's perfect, thank God

Newspapers demand a lot of qualities from subs. They're never all found in one man, and that's a mercy. If they ever were he'd stay about a fortnight and then become chairman of Ford's or Prime Minister, and we'd all have £100 cars and no income tax. But that's no good reason for not listing some of the qualities that are desirable in a sub.

Herewith the Compleat Sub:

The good sub has a sharp news sense, but is not concerned with news as an abstraction, or with his own particular prejudices or interests. The first will lead him into forgetting the kind of reader he is aiming at, and the second into only getting excited about stories emanating in Central Africa or dealing with the Chelsea set, according to his individual weakness. His news sense will be related to the newspaper he is working on, so that he can snatch from a mass of copy the intro that will excite his reader.

In some cases he will have to lean over backwards and cultivate a Pavlovian reaction, so that he positively salivates when he sees the words workers' solidarity while subbing on the *Morning Star,* or the Battle of Britain when he moves to the *Sunday Express,* or homosexuality, abortion, penal reform, race relations, and incest when he's doing a Saturday

---

*Such as the chairman having an obsession with the subject, or the editor being in love with the actress mentioned in the third paragraph.

casual stint on *The Observer*. There is nothing degrading about this, any more than there is in writing a TV serial which people actually want to watch.

Privately the sub may be completely cynical about the way the story is done, or doubt its comparative value as against other stories, or even question whether it ought to be in the newspaper at all. But professionally his job is to produce the best possible story *within his terms of reference*. When he gets further up the ladder, of course, he'll be able to question the terms of reference, and even get them changed. But he won't get there if he spends his time arguing instead of subbing.

The good sub has an orderly mind and a cool head, so that when he is faced with great wodges of copy coming from all directions he will be able to cope without panicking. Only an orderly mind can handle a running story about an air crash in Yugoslavia when Reuter, AP, UPI and two stringers are running good and strong, a staff man is due on the scene at midnight, and seventeen local correspondents all over the British Isles are sending in backgrounders on survivors.

But this kind of mind is essential in lesser situations — the putting together of a messy court story, or knocking sense into an account of a council meeting written by an inexperienced reporter. Unless the facts are clear and in sequence in the sub's mind, or at any rate on his copy pad, they won't be clear and in sequence in the newspaper.

The good sub has a good general knowledge, and that means really *general*, for a sub can afford few blind spots. The question "Who is Debbie Harry?" may raise a laugh in the High Court, but it's not funny in a newspaper. The sub must know about pop singers and Cabinet Ministers, film stars and company bosses, night club owners and chairmen of Royal Commissions.

This knowledge must be up to date and relate to his newspaper. If he is working on a pop star with a youthful circulation the name Tom Jones must mean to him an ageing pop singer first, and a film second, and the original Fielding book a rather poor third. If he is on *The Guardian* the situation will be reversed. But he must be aware of all three.

"Book learning" is not the greatest source of this kind of knowledge. Reading newspapers is. This involves a wide range of newspapers, but particularly those in the same spectrum as the one the sub is working on. Doing this will not only keep him up to date on events, but will give him a sensitivity about the people whose very names are news. If the 37th name on a list of air crash victims is M Streep, he must immediately demand to know if he has a dead star on his hands or whether he is dealing with the M Streep who runs the tripe and cowheel stall in Elmstead Woods market.

Another good rule for the sub who wants to keep himself in touch with people and things in the news, and pick up a lot of information into the bargain: **WATCH THE TELLY.**

Apart from the fact that TV produces most of our great idol-figures, and is an incessant topic of conversation on the rush-hour trains from both Virginia Water and St Mary Cray, it is also a useful source of ideas and techniques.

A sub-editor working on a morning paper *must* known how The News at Ten handles things, and what kind of news it handles. But it is also important to have seen all the Top 20 programmes at least once — because the people the sub is subbing for will have done so, and professionally at least he's got to share their lives. No man can hope to fire on all cylinders with a story about Mrs Mary Whitehouse if he's not watched Channel 4 flashing its naughty bits.

The good sub is obsessed with accuracy, for even the smallest mistake will damage the newspaper. One name spelt wrongly, even though it belongs to some unimportant chap, will bring the paper into ill repute.

In a later chaper I go thoroughly into the question of checking facts. Here I only add one comment: In a sub-editor, accuracy is more important than genius.

The good sub is able to work fast when the occasion arises, which will probably be quite often. The sub is tied to the clock. The perfect story means nothing if it misses the edition. It is worse than useless if it delays the edition to the extent of missing trains and planes. The sub will do himself a power of good. The technique is simple, and involves cultivating disastrously late.

Yet every late story presents the sub with a great opportunity to do himself a power of good. The technique is simple, and involves cultivating a capacity to know *how much* he can do and still get the story up on time.

He does just that and no more. Then he comes to the second and vital stage. He determinedly goes back to it on a later edition and does the polished job he had hoped to do in the first place.

But all the time he must keep an eye on the clock. This is the sacred thing. Sub-editing is the job in which clock-watching is a virtue.

The good sub can write a bright, workmanlike headline. This aspect of the sub's job I explore in detail in another chapter. Here it is enough to say that the sub who learns to turn in a good heading and turn it in quickly, is doing himself a great service. If the chief sub finds himself wasting his valuable time even trying to think up alternatives because he is vaguely dissatisfied with the sub's attempts, then over a period of time he is going to get vaguely irritated.

The good sub has some knowledge of law as it applies to newspapers. This doesn't mean that he is able to quote paragraph four of subsection vi of section 47 of whatever Act it is. If he can do that he has got a mind which is legalistic rather than journalistic, and should start reading for the Bar forthwith.

But he should and must know what he can say without actually libelling somebody, or getting the editor hauled up before the Bar of the House of Commons. He must particularly beware of getting his editor nicked for contempt of court.

I remember once submitting a rather dicey story to Mr Howard Sabin, who was at the time offering legal advice to Associated Newspapers but soon afterward moved on and prosecuted the Great Train Robbers. He brought the copy back to me with the wry remark: "Far be it from me to interfere with promotion prospects in the *Daily Mail,* but if you publish this the editor will surely go to jail."

One thing's for sure: the chap who'd perpetrated the contempt would have been a non-runner in the promotion race that followed. A sub who costs the newspaper hard cash in libel damages is never really forgiven, by the company accountants anyway. A sub who lands the editor inside can consider himself a write-off.

The good sub maintains a sense of excitement about change. Most subs react well to changes in the news — to the kind of situation in which a running story has to be re-introed six times between editions because of later developments. But the good sub reacts equally well to the changes that to him do not seem so necessary or obvious: the shuffling of stories from one page to another, the changing of angles, the trimming and the extending.

He recognises that the executives who are making these changes are not doing it for the hell of it. After all, it's making work for them too. They have only one motive — that they think the paper will be the better for it. They may be right or wrong, and they may have at the back of their minds the thought that if anyone collects the credit it's going to be them, but the basic urge is the right one. Resistance to change, whatever the motive for it, should be absolutely alien to anyone described (as the court reports say) as a journalist.

The good sub knows what length his story will make. When asked for 9 inches of 8 points he does not turn in 15 inches. This length business is purely a matter of practice and determination to estimate accurately. After a while it ceases to be necessary to count words or even lines of copy. A quick run of the eye down the folios is enough to convert the copy into column inches of ordinary body matter.

The sub whose cast-offs are consistently bad is unpopular all round. He particularly enrages the stone subs and everyone on the mechanical side. The sub whose stories *always* have to be cut or *always* have to be brassed out is wasting time — not his own, but that of his colleagues, who could be better employed.

The good sub approaches all stories with a healthy cynicism, and not only about facts and the way they are interpreted. He exercises a particular care about "scandal" and hard luck stories and works on the premise that in 99 cases out of 100 there is another side to the story and it is the newspaper's absolute duty to give it.

Local authorities, while they may occasionally be slow and stupid and pompous and obsessed with their own bureaucratic procedure, on the whole don't evict penniless mothers of seven without some good reason. Investigation is quite likely to show that not only has Mum not paid the rent for 18 months but that she is living with a West Indian pot-peddler and has put her children in the gravest moral danger.

Likewise headmistresses, though some may be arrogant or frustrated, don't on the whole bar girls from school unless there's smoke which is likely to burst into flame at any moment. Behind the apparently trivial matter of the fifth-former and her engagement ring ("School bars Sandra over ring") may well lie a more serious and unprintable story of a wayward wench disrupting the whole place.

A classic example of the failure of newspapers generally to exercise a justified cynicism about a one-sided story was provided by the saga of Police Constable Alexander Archibald, who was shot in the spine as he tried to arrest a gunman and later transferred to a CID desk job.

Most newspapers seized with joy at the story of the hero "sacked" with a small pension. But within days the other side of the story was told: that PC Archibald was bored with his desk job and wanted to leave the police force and start life afresh as a publican. Only the amount of pension was in dispute.

The sub must be sure that he knows both sides of the story, however much he has to pester and nag the news room to get both sides. If after pestering and nagging he is still left with gaps, he must point them out and let someone else carry the can.

All kinds of disputes, particularly strikes, call for this same cautiously cynical approach. The good sub is careful not to take any statement at its face value, and keep a sharp ear open for the sound of the axe grinding.

The good sub does one thing superbly well, preferably (from his point of view) better than anyone else on the table. He may know all about show biz or politics, or write a superb caption, or handle a complex running story so fast and accurately that every one else is astonished. He may just be the man who never makes any mistakes in the rainfall figures and the tide tables, so that the editor is not forever answering letters of complaint from the publicity department at Torquay or from chaps who get stuck on mudbanks in the Thames. But if he is spectacularly good at one thing a lot of failings in other directions will be forgiven him.

The good sub avoids being deliberately miserable. That doesn't mean deliberately turning bad news into good, but it does mean not going out of your way to depress the reader by putting the worst possible interpretation on an item of news.

Regrettably, some newspapers make a habit of it — I have one in front of me that has a page lead about "miserable" exam pass rates (the small print says they've improved); another chastising the readers for *still* driving carelessly (the Christmas accident rate had dropped dramatically); a third about the "spectre of crime" ruining the festive season (its misery index is padded out with accidents, suicides, glue sniffing, smuggling and what could well have been a death from natural causes); and a fourth "huge drought threat horror" which says way down the story that the dams are filling up nicely, thank you.

Subs, like newspapers, should remember the tradition of killing the messenger who bears the bad news.

The good sub can write clearly, crisply and concisely. I have left this till last, although it is clearly the most important, and overshadows all the others, because this aptitude is so dependent on some of the qualities mentioned earlier. It involves, for example, coolness, orderliness and a sense of the value of one fact against that of another.

For how to achieve this essential clarity, crispness and conciseness — read on.

How to get 10 out of 10

After that frightening list of qualities, some thoughts about the qualities required in the finished story.

I suggest a series of questions which every sub could well ask himself about each story before he drops it wearily in the chief sub's basket. And don't tell me that no sub has got time to ask himself questions. Sometimes he has, and then it's often a salutary experience. In any case, it's useful in a quiet moment to go back over stories subbed earlier to see how they stand up to the test. For unless they *do* stand up, and unless you get the right answers to all the questions, then it's not a well-subbed story.

1. ARE THE FACTS RIGHT? Are you absolutely sure that the Munro-Lucas-Tooth family have two hyphens in their name? Are you confident that it's Newcastle-under-Lyme that has hyphens and Newcastle upon Tyne that doesn't? Was the last Lewisham rail crash really as long ago as 1957 — or was it 1959? Don't look now, but does Pergamon Press have one *m* or two?

2. ARE THERE ANY LOOSE ENDS? Have you started the reader off on a line of thought and left him dangling there? Is every sequence brought to a proper conclusion? Are there any facts missing which are necessary to a complete story — or, if there are, have you already put inquiries in hand?

It's astonishingly easy to miss a vital point unless you check back over your work with that in mind.

I remember when I was a young sub on the *News Chronicle* in Manchester doing a tear-jerking, soul-searing rewrite from 90 pages of a PA court report. Strong men wept all over the building. Congratulations came from the most unexpected quarters. The editor did everything short of giving me a rise. Then the next day the copy-taster took me aside, put a grandfatherly hand on my shoulder, and said:

"It was a great job you did — *but what was the result of the case?*"

In my enthusiasm for the musical arrangements I'd dropped the key line in the lyric.

3. IS EVERYTHING CLEAR? Has everything that needs explaining been explained? Will the story mean something to even the dimmest reader? (and there are a lot of dim readers about). I've just been reading a tale about butter oil. *What is butter oil?* I didn't know when I started and I don't know now, and that's not good enough. What is worse I suspect the sub didn't know and didn't ask. Beware of butter oil and gudgeon pins and hypertension and all their brothers and sisters. Somebody, somewhere, won't know what you're on about unless you explain.

4. DOES IT FLOW LIKE HONEY, in Christiansen's phrase, or does it stick in the craw? Anything that causes the reader to pause, even momentarily, is bad. The sequence should be perfect, the facts blindingly simple. Nothing should be there that jars, or causes the reader to look back to an earlier paragraph.

5. DOES IT MAKE ANY UNNECESSARY DEMANDS ON THE CUSTOMER? It ought not to. An unexplained reference to the HNP in a story from South Africa *is* an unnecessary demand, because in spite of the barrage of references to the HNP there are still customers who need a phrase which tells, even vaguely, what the HNP is. Surveys show that most members of the Cabinet are unknown to most readers, and therefore, idiotic as it may see, it is necessary to attach their chain of office to them every time they are mentioned.

6. CAN IT BE SIMPLIFIED? If it *can* be simplified further there is something wrong with it.

The operating sub may find more questions to suit his own market. If he does, good luck to him, and I'd be glad to hear from him. At any rate, let him note these six.

For God's sake care – about the basic things

THE really basic mechanics of subbing can be learned in a night and after that it's the talent that counts. As Lord Mancroft has remarked, all men are born equal, but quite a few of them eventually get over it. The good sub, of course, will not be content with the basics, and having once mastered them he will expand his interests into overlapping fields such as pictures, typography and design.

This chapter is intended to cover merely the essentials — the things a sub really needs to know, plus some rules for handling particular kinds of stories which will inevitably drop on his desk at one time or another.

Keep it clean

To mark up copy for the Printer the sub need know no more than the body sizes in use and the system of marking them used in the newspaper he is working for. They will be known either by straight point sizes, which is becoming increasingly common, or by the old names which have been handed down over the years. These are the names and the sizes most commonly in use:

Pica, pronounced pi-kah	12 point
Long primer, pronounced primmer, written lp	10 point
Bourgeois, pronounced burjoyce, written bour	9 point
Brevier, pronounced brev-eer, written brev	8 point
Minion, written min	7 point
Nonpareil, pronounced non-prul, written nonp	6 point
Ruby	5½ point
Pearl	5 point

Even in offices which retain the old names, sizes above pica are known by their points measurement. This is calculated on the body depth of the type face, not the letter itself, and is approximately 72 points to the inch.

Whatever the office form, there is a good rule to apply in the marking up of copy. It is this:

SAY AS MUCH AS IS NEEDED TO MAKE THE MEANING ABSOLUTELY CLEAR — AND NO MORE.

Suppose, for example, the main body matter of the newspaper is 8 point Jubilee single column full out. It is unnecessary and time wasting to write on each folio

8 pt Jubilee × 1 full out

or even

8 Jub × 1 f o

because it is highly unlikely that the copy would appear in the page set in 8 point Century Schoolbook nut e/s, or in 8 point Plantin pica each side, even if the full details were not present. It is quite adequate to write

8 × 1

and anything else is unnecessary fuss.

Similarly, if you suddenly get a rush of indented italics to the head, it is enough to mark the offending paragraph

8 ital × 1 em e/s

and then mark the next paragraph

8 rom × 1 full

without the additional confusion of preceding it with

end 8 ital × 1 em e/s

The fewer the instructions are, consistent with clarity, the more likely the story is to turn up set correctly, and the more time the sub has available to deal with other important matters.

This minimal marking is one of the main contributions the sub can make to the compositor's delight: Clean copy. If the sub is doing his job properly there will be handwritten marks on most (though not all) folios of copy. These should be as clear as humanly possible. Medical-type handwriting may be forgivable on prescriptions, but it's not on subbed copy. Bad handwriting leads to setting errors, which lead to readers' corrections, which lead to late pages.

Plates 1 and 2 show examples of clean copy, one a first folio needing few marks, and the other heavily subbed but perfectly legible.

Certain other things are needed on copy other than typographical instructions and changes in text made by the sub.

There's a catch in it somewhere

The most important of these is the catchline. Without proper attention to the "catch", and this very quickly becomes automatic, the most almighty chaos can arise. The catchline's function is to identify beyond any doubt which story is being dealt with, and its part in the sequence. In hard copy — that is, on paper, not video screen — it should appear in the top right-hand corner of every folio, and consist of one key word followed by a folio number.

A good rule for the catchline is:

KEEP IT SHORT, KEEP IT RELEVANT, KEEP IT CLEAN — AND DON'T BE FUNNY, BECAUSE A CATCHLINE IS A SERIOUS BUSINESS.

To take these points in sequence:

Keep it short because it saves time. It is easier to write HAT 3 than it is to write MILLINERY 3. It is also easier, if a folio of copy goes temporarily astray, for the man on the desk to call for SICK 5 than it is to cry PNEUMOCONIOSIS 5.

Keep it relevant because that way it is easier to find the metal when there are corrections to be done. I recall a chap on the *News Chronicle* who caused endless confusion by catchlining every story of which he disapproved with a minor obscenity. When the old codger concerned was finally faced with a complete ban on a dirty word he immediately retaliated substituting another meaning the same.

This sort of nonsense catchline should and must be avoided. If a Corrector of the Press is wandering about apparently aimlessly crying out loud "Have you got a story about CHICKEN?" he is likely to find it if it concerns an outbreak of fowl pest in Norfolk, but not if it's a story about the Conservative candidate for Accrington refusing to take part in a debate with his Labour opponent.

It is also necessary to avoid catchlines that are TOO RELEVANT. The reason is simple: Unless everybody is following the same rule then there is a likelihood of the same catchline appearing twice, with the result that two stories are mixed up on the random, or the wrong headline gets on a story. It is clearly madness on the night of a general election to catchline any story ELECTION, because there are so many stories on that theme, or on the night a plane falls on the Hammersmith Palais to use the word CRASH, because there's a crashing night ahead. But there are also certain words to avoid at all times, simply because there are so many stories associated with them:

CRASH	JOBS	PLANE
DEATH	JUDGE	STRIKE
DIVORCE	MP	WIFE

There are dozens more. The important thing is — if it's likely to be on someone else's story, don't use it.

Keep it clean because you don't know whose hands it will get into outside the editorial department, and because there is always the danger that a catchline will get into the page. Get a divorce story about a man with seven mistresses and it seems the most natural thing in the world to catchline it CRUMPET. But think not only of the little girl who is crediting the local correspondent with his payment, but also of the local preacher who is in charge of the linage department and filled with a nauseating urge to protect her. Think even more of the embarrassment if the paper appeared with the catchline looking for all the world like a crosshead — and that's happened more than once. He would have to be a valuable sub-editor to survive such a happening.

Don't be funny, for reasons covered in the point already made above. It may seem amusing to get a story about the Prime Minister and catchline it LOUSE. But nobody will be able to find which story it refers to, and the local preacher mentioned earlier will turn out to be chairman of his ward political party and make a formal protest to the union.

Other points to note about catchlines:

1. Some offices make a practice of numbering the heading BROWN 1 or whatever, with the next folio numbered 1½. It seems a bit eccentric to me, but if that's the office style, then follow it.

2. Catchlines which a sub requires to be set and left on the story until it is put in the page must be preceded by the words SET CATCH. The word to be set must *not* be ringed, because that gives the composing department a complete escape if anything goes wrong — in theory no ringed words are set. This usually concerns stories or paragraphs which must appear —

> set catch — MUST
> set catch — MUST PAR
> set catch — MUST PAR ENDS

or in uncuttable stuff

> set catch — DON'T CUT

or in organising a special proof distribution —

> set catch — EARLY PROOFS TO NIGHT ED, CHIEF SUB,
> LAWYER AND PRIVATE EYE.

This way the comps have no excuse at all for dropping you in it.

3. Stories must not in any circumstances be catchlined KILL or DEAD. These are words which denote that the metal has been or is to be junked, and if a story is found lying on the random with one of these catchlines and gets thrown away it's nobody fault but the sub's. These catchlines are particularly dangerous if written on revise proofs.

Similar, though less forceful, arguments can be advanced against using any other word which has other meanings in relation to a newspaper office, such as TOP or SHORT. It would of course be asking for trouble to send up the 10 point paragraph of a story on mini-skirts with the catchline MIN 1.

4. If a story requires an insert in copy still in the sub's hands it is not necessary to renumber all through. It is adequate to slip in a folio marked.
SWEETS 4½
providing that folio 4-ends with the note
SWEETS 4½ FOLLOWS
to avoid confusion on the random.

5. Some offices adopt a system of letters plus numbers on running stories; in this, following the Press Association on major Parliamentary events. This involves, for example, ending the intro on say a big debate with the words
A SECTION FOLLOWS
and then dealing with the Prime Minister's speech as A1, A2 and so on. This would end with
B SECTION FOLLOWS
and the Leader of the Opposition would be numbered B1, B2, *ad infinitum* or *ad nauseum* or something.

One final point: it is always useful to keep a log of the catchlines you've used on the current issue. It means you don't have to search your memory if you need to send up an insert or add.

Get it up, lads

There are times in the lives of most subs when they get an hour to devote to moulding and polishing a beautiful tale, and those to whom it never happens wish it did. But generally the sub is required to combine a good job of work with speed, and when it comes to the crunch the speed has to take priority over the polish. A good rule to operate most of the time:
GET IT UP, LADS — YOU'VE GOT A TRAIN TO CATCH.
Nine times out of ten someone is waiting for the story even before you've started to sub it. There are Linotype operators on the slate, and that makes them very angry if they're paid on piece rates. There's a hole at the foot of Page Seven which the stone-hand won't make up till he knows the length of your triple-up. There's a Printer developing the galloping nadgers because he knows the paper is going to be late again.

Because of all this it's desirable to get into the habit of sending longish stories to the composing room a bit at a time. You'll have to do it anyway if you get an urgent running story like a rail crash, and doing it regularly is good practice.

Here it becomes important to log not only the catchlines but also the folio numbers that have gone up. There's always a danger in the rush of changing catchlines in mid-story, and of losing track of the numbering. It's bad enough to get two folios numbered RAIL 9, but even more chaos-making if one is numbered RAIL 9 and the next one TRAIN 9.

Before starting to send up a story a bit at a time it is vital to be absolutely clear what the sequence is. A minute spent jotting down notes on a complex story is saved many times over later on. There's no point in doing a running story if it's going to be followed by adds, inserts, cuts and bits of resetting. The only justification for these things is a later development or later instructions which affect the story.

Another useful rule to apply is this, **IF IT'S COMPLICATED, SEND IT UP FIRST.** Straight setting across a stock measure can be eaten up by the composing room. It can be blanked for in the page. But the complex things, particularly if they involve a different part of the composing room, eat up the valuable time.

Thus if you have a straight story with a tie-in box — do the box first. It not only has to be set, probably in a bastard measure, but with hot metal it then has to go over to the case to have the rules cut and mitred. If you have a multi-column headline in some odd shape, including more than one type, do it before the story, because it will take longer to make up than the story will to set. If you've got a caption that goes in a pierce, give it priority (unless you're working on a paste-up for web-offset) because they'll probably set three stories in the time it will take to cut and pack it. With *anything* complicated — do it first, because that's where the delay will lie.

If you're using old-fashioned hot-metal setting **NEVER USE TWO SIZES OF TYPE ON ONE FOLIO OF COPY.** If you do it will have to be cut up by the copy desk before it can be distributed to the operators, who would rightly take a poor view of changing over their machine in mid-folio just because the sub wasn't doing his job properly.

Know also the limitations of your own setting department. If, for example, it has 8 point Vogue Bold on only one machine and you choose that type for ten matching 2-inch captions it's going to be quite a while before you get the metal. One man has got to do the whole job, and the corrections have to wait for that machine to become clear again.

Don't ask the comps to mix roman, italic and bold in one paragraph unless you've got a lot of time and they've got a lot of staff to spare. The roman will be duplexed with *either* italic *or* bold on the machine, and to introduce a third variant will involve having a separate bar set on another machine and cutting it in by hand.

Be cautious about mixing case and keyboard setting if the edition if drawing near. One of the most useful ways of breaking long stories into sections, or setting out nibs, is to do the first word of the par in a contrasting face such as 12 point Century Extended lower case, or 14 Medium Condensed Sans caps, inset into the top line. But this may involve two operators, one on the Linotype or Intertype and one on the Ludlow at the other end of the room, and possibly a third man carting the bits of metal to and fro and cutting them in. Do this kind of thing, yes — but watch the clock.

Generally speaking, don't attempt more than you've got time for. There are, of course, occasions when you've got to push you luck for the sake of producing a first-class newspaper. It happens on every edition of every good, lively newspaper — that's the way they stay good, lively newspapers. The constant striving to do it better is what is needed. But DON'T on EVERY story bite off more than you can chew. Don't attempt a complete rewrite ten minutes before close-copy time. Don't change course and up-end a story if it's already late. Chance your arm, if it's for the good of the paper, but don't risk you neck.

The same principles apply to rejigs on proof. If they've got to be done because of later developments or changed pages get them into the hands of the Printer as soon as possible. But with rejigs that amount to cleaning up, polishing or turning a story around because you've changed your mind, don't try too much. If half the story is out of the page when the page should have left the composing room you'll get no thanks from anybody.

Of course, it's different with an electronic system, but more of that later.

The proof of the pudding

It is essential that marks on proofs should be clean and legible, and the sub must know the basic ones. I won't go into great detail here, because this is *The simple subs book* and not *The complicated proof readers book*. The points that follow are those that are really necessary to the sub.

1. The only marks in the text should be those indicating the *place* to which the correction refers. The corrections themselves should be written in the margin. They should never be written sideways because this puts too much strain on the chap setting the corrections and one dirty proof is likely to be followed by another.

2. If more than one correction occurs in any line the correction should be divided between the left and right margins, in left to right order.

3. Each correction should be followed by a concluding mark, which is a simple oblique stroke /.

4. To delete a word, line or paragraph strike it through clearly and in the margin write the delete mark, which is a Greek *d* linked to a concluding mark —

δ7

5. If you change your mind and want to restore any material, put a line of dots under the word or words and in the margin write *stet*.

6. When you insert something don't draw wiggly lines all over the proof. Simply place an insertion mark —

λ

in the text, write the new matter in the margin and follow it with a concluding mark /.

7. To change words to italic draw a straight line under them and write *ital* in the margin. To change to bold draw a wobbly line and write *bold* in the margin. To change to roman *ring* the words and write *rom*.

Changing words to caps is more difficult because theoretically three lines should be drawn under them. This is all very well in book setting 10 on 12 point but not so easy with 7 point solid on a damp bit of newsprint. I've found that most offices will accept either one line or a ringed word with *caps* written in the margin.

8. It may sometimes be necessary to indicate a wrong fount, usually at the last minute, although this is usually left to the readers. This is done by ringing the character and writing *w.f.* in the margin.

9. Underlining is indicated by drawing a line under the words and writing *underline* in the margin. Some offices use *fine score*.

10. To close up the words, such as when headmaster has split and the style is to make it one word, the linking characters

⌒
‿

are used in the text and repeated in the margin.

11. To insert space the insertion mark (see point 6) is used in the text and the space mark

#

in the margin. Extra spacing between lines or paragraphs is indicated by

>

between the lines and by the space mark in the margin. To reduce or equalise space a vertical stroke is drawn between the words and

written in the margin.

12. Words to be transposed are linked in the text by the transposition mark

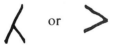

and the letters *trs* are written in the margin.

13. A new paragraph is indicated by the sign

in the text and *n.p.* in the margin. The running on of two paragraphs is indicated by linking them

and writing *run on* or *r.o.* in the margin.

14. A missing word or line is indicated by the insertion marks

and *out see copy* in the margin.

15. Punctuation is inserted by using the first insertion mark in the text and these symbols in the margin

Note that the full point and colon are ringed, but the semi-colon, question mark, exclamation mark, parenthesis, hyphen, dash, apostrophe and quote marks are followed by the concluding mark.

There are many other marks, such as those for raising and lowering lines, inverting type, and even for substituting inferior or superior figures, but those I've dealt with are reasonably adequate for the sub's job.

One further point needs to be strongly: **BEWARE OF WORKING ON DIRTY PROOFS.** If there is a mistake, particularly in a figure, it is quite likely to be corrected on the reader's proof and restored as a result of a sub making marks on an uncorrected proof. After that it's pure chance whether it gets put right again.

In a newspaper producing more than one edition it is vital that after the first edition, rejigs of early stories should be done on page proofs. Apart from not accounting for corrections, a galley proof rejig won't take any account of cuts that have been done on the stone or those made by an enraged night editor on first setting eyes on the subbed version of a story.

If it's style, stick to it

Style, in newspaper terms, means the practice laid down by a particular office to ensure consistency and accuracy. In *Doing it in style** I defined it as covering three main fields:

1. Forms of spelling, abbreviations and contractions which are generally acceptable and adopted as the newspaper's practice.

2. Forms to use in such matters as titles, military ranks, and government, financial and church affairs.

3. Accepted standards in the construction of a newspaper story, contributing to the one true test of its success: *Is it easily read?*

Though I suggested forms which could be adopted generally, it remains true that a lot of offices have certain rules which if not peculiar to them are at any rate peculiar.

Right unto its death, the London *Evening News,* for example, spelt *today* as to-day, which is correct but somewhat archaic, and looked particularly odd when in headings.

One national newspaper (and wild horses wouldn't drag the name of the *Daily Telegraph* from my lips) banned the words commuter, millionaire, Tory and walkie-talkie, which seemed to me to carry the old ostrich habit a bit far.

Several local papers I know insist on abbreviating Councillor not as *Coun* which is bad enough, but as *Cllr,* which is worse.

But whatever idiosyncracies occur in an individual newspaper's style sheet it's the sub's duty to follow it. Take to heart the rule: **KNOW YOUR STYLE SHEET — AND ACT ON IT.**

You may think it odd to write *head-master* with a hyphen in the middle, or *head master* as two words, but if you write *headmaster* and the comp sets

*Pergamon Press, 1968

it, that simply means another line of correction to be done when the reader's proof comes out.

You may be driven mad (as I am) by the trend summed up in this letter:

"DISALLOWING initial capital letters is all very well, but it has made The Sunday Times harder to read. I know instantly what 'the House' is, but 'the house' does not signal Westminster to me at all.

"This editorial quirk is leading to ambiguity. The 'television act of 1953' (Books last week) could be something by Morecambe and Wise instead of the Television Act passed by Parliament.

"I am diverted by comical irrelevance. I never knew of Sir John Donaldson's demotion to being a baker before, but you label him the 'master of the rolls' ".

I think it's confusing and makes life harder for the reader, but the sub is stuck with it till he becomes editor and can change it.

Points on which many newspapers lay down firm rules include these:

Abbreviations	Compound words
Addresses	Dates and figures
Anglicised words	Punctuation
Christian names	Titles
Collective nouns	

In addition there may be a list of banned or disliked words and phrases.

To take the sketchy list above as a guideline, these are the things a sub could be expected to know, preferably without looking them up.

WHETHER it's permissible to contract the rank lieutenant-commander, where it's permissible to contract it, and whether the permitted contraction is Lt Cdr or Lieut Cdr or Lt.Cmdr. If the lieutenant-commander were a Member of Parliament the sub would also need to know whether the abbreviation took full points or not — M.P. or MP? If he were also a magistrate the sub would need to know whether the newspaper practice was to add J.P. (or JP) after the name. Some do and some don't. The possible permutations are vast —

> Lieutenant-Commander Bokes, M.P.
> Lieut-Cmdr Bokes. MP, JP
> Lt.Cdr. Bokes, M.P.
> Lieut-Commander Bokes, M.P., J.P.

and so on.

WHETHER addresses are abbreviated — St or St. for Street — and if so whether they are hyphenated to the previous word; if road numbers or postal districts are to be given.

WHETHER certain anglicised words like blase, debris and expose should be set in roman or italic and which of them should retain their accents. I personally take the view that if it's so foreign that it needs to be in italic it has no business appearing in a popular newspaper.

WHETHER the newspaper allows the use of Christian names in chatty stories, and where the line is drawn. It is permissible to refer to a char who comes up on the pools as just Maggie, when it's quite apparent that we can't call the chairman of GEC Arnold? For that matter, is it permitted to say Philip in headlines, when His Royal Highness Prince Philip Duke of Edinburgh is meant? Many newspapers have stern rules on a matter like this.

WHETHER collective nouns are always singular, always plural, or modified for sense. *Is* Blankton Press making a bid for Penguins, or *are* they? Does style call for "The Government *are* ruining the country" or for "The Government *is* doing a great job". Does the newspaper apply the rules for news stories to sport as well? (Most newspapers which treat collective nouns as singular make an exception for football and cricket teams and so on.)

WHETHER certain compound words are hyphenated, set as one word, or split in two. It is possible to lay down some principles which make a list of words unnecessary, but some newspapers *do* have a list and it has to be followed.

WHETHER dates are set November 19, November 19th, 19 November or 19th November, whether it is permissible to abbreviate the month, and if so whether September is contracted to Sept (as by most newspapers) or Sep (as by most international organisations)? In numbers, whether ten is spelt out or set as 10, and what rule applies if numbers above and below ten appear in one sequence.

WHETHER the office concerned is pedantic about punctuation, or whether it inclines to test its efficiency purely by readability, and whether there is a down on dashes and ellipses.

WHETHER there are rules about the use of titles which go beyond the matter of correctness. Is it the rule, for example, that at the first mention of an earl, he should be called "earl", but thereafter referred to as "lord"? Does some maniac proprietor insist that his favourite duke should always get the description "His Grace"? Must our heir to the throne always be called the Prince of Wales, or can we relax sometimes and call him Prince Charles?

Remember that these rules of house style are not entirely a matter of correctness. If they were, the style sheet would not be necessary. Their main motive is consistency: to ensure that a paper doesn't change tense in mid-sentence; or say organise and organize in the same column; or use sea-shore in one part of the paper and seashore in another.

Cast off — and sail ahead

The newspaper term "casting-off" can be defined as calculating how much a given amount of copy will make in a given size, type and measure — assuming, of course, that he doesn't have a computer to do it for him. The request "Give us a cast-off, Fred" means "How long will your story be?"

An ability to cast off accurately is highly regarded in a sub, particularly if he is working to tight spaces on a tabloid newspaper. An experienced man can run his eye or pencil quickly down a story, give a rapid estimate, and not be more than half an inch out in a 10-inch story.

But this needs a great deal of practice and anyone reasonably new to the job will find it well worth while to do a simple space count table. The most straightforward way to do this is to find the average number of words the basic body type gives to the inch in the usual permutations — full out, nut each side, em each side, full and one nut right — and do a rough word count on the copy.

After a while it becomes easy to do a fairly accurate guesstimate. You may find, for example, that five lines of typewritten copy are roughly equal to ten lines (one inch) of 7 point full. It's possible on this basis to whip through several folios of copy, making rapid mental adjustments for cut lines and matter written in.

Some subs who have a good reputation for casting off stories for length fail when it comes to intros. In many local papers the most terrible abortions appear — one and a half lines across two columns carrying 12 inches of single column matter (which is bottom-heavy) or eight lines of 10 point across three, which is unreadable.

On the standard broadsheet column, 10 point is needed to provide reasonably legible double-column setting, and 12 point for setting across three. In each case the sub should follow the advice in the old shaving cream ad: **NOT TOO LITTLE, NOT TOO MUCH, BUT JUST RIGHT.**

"Just right" is about four or five lines. This gives a reasonable balance between top-heaviness and puniness.

Note how unreadable this intro is from a purely typographical point of view:

WHITEHALL has warned all Army and RAF units in the country that a breathalyser conviction in a civil court will rate as a "serious offence". Under Queen's Regulations, all civil offences, except minor ones like parking, must be reported to commanding officers. A conviction against an officer must be notified to the Ministry of Defence which, if the case is very grave, may cashier him or ask him to resign.

Then notice the unbalanced effect of the too-short par, which leaves the drop uncovered.

A POLICE trap led to four Britons facing drug charges here today.

Here, an ideal length for a two-column intro:

A CABLE calling for negotiations within a week on South Arabia's independence, due later this month, was sent to Mr Septimus Mortimer-Brown, the Foreign Secretary, yesterday. It came from the National Liberation Front, victor in the struggle for power in South Arabia.

The sub should know, and if necessary keep in writing, the average number of words he needs to achieve this in every permutation his newspaper uses, whether it's 10 point Ionic across two or 18 point Futura Bold across three. It's only *part* of the sub's job to get the perfect intro from a verbal point of view. If it's unreadable or looks bad it won't have the desired effect.

Similar principles apply to single column intros. Here brevity is the rule. A long par of 12 point single column is hard to read. If it's followed by a long par of 10 point and then a long par of 8 point then the customer is faced with a hard task.

Compare the comparative readability of these two settings, and note the crisper, newsier appearance of that with short pars:

A GRENADE was thrown through the window of a Jewish minister's home yesterday.

It exploded, wrecking a downstairs room.

The Rev Bernard Braunstein, 48, his wife and their six children, aged between 2 and 22, were asleep upstairs at the time.

The grenade, a Mills type used by British troops in both world wars, exploded in the lounge of Mr Braunstein's home in Chatsworth Road, Brighton.

THE allegation that bus inspectors had "leaned over backwards" to help during the busmen's overtime ban was made by Mr J Conley, Secretary of the Municipal Passenger Branch of the Transport and General Worker's Union, following the midnight meeting of the men.

Mr Conley said "Due to the fact that the management have flatly refused to withdraw its inspectors from performing road duties, we have been compelled to withdraw our labour, as from tonight for one week, unless the management in the meantime are willing to negotiate with us."

Mr Conley went on, "The inspectors have been instructed to resume their normal duties. That means, in fact, that they take over buses in emergencies. In normal circumstances they can take over buses in emergencies until the crews arrive, but we claim that these were not normal circumstances, and during the ban they have still been doing road duties."

They show that it's almost as important to watch the cast-offs as it is to watch the words.

Shorts are short, and that's that

Accurate cast-offs are particularly important when it comes to shorts. Many newspapers, probably most now, have a system of shorts graduated by length and headline size. This is by far the best way of handling the o and s of news which break up the paper typographically and give it a variety and vigour.

A typical system might be:

A-head: One line 14 point heading, 4-6 lines of copy
B-head: One line 18 point, 6-9 lines of copy
C-head: Two lines 18 point, 9-12 lines of copy
D-head: Two lines 24 point, 10-14 lines of copy.

When a system like this operates the sub should strive to keep well within the maximum number of lines, otherwise the short will look unbalanced and have a slabby appearance instead of providing an efficient breaker.

Unless all headlines are ranged left the two-liners should have a fairly-full top line and a shorter second line:

Brown flays Thomson

Harold flays Gladys

Pyramids or squared-off headlines should be avoided

Thomson flays Brown

Harold flays Gladys Mary

Label headlines should not be used on two-liners, although with one-line headings the good label is preferable to the dull heading containing a verb. Here are two examples, the first showing splendid ingenuity, the second something of a cliché but one calculated to amuse a lot of people:

London-on-Sea

Greater London Council is to develop an overspill area for 300 London families at Bognor Regis.

The Midas touch

A man from Hythe, Southampton, has won £2,287 at a Bournemouth casino in a bingo competition. His name: Mr Golden.

These shorts would have been far less effective if an attempt had been made to *contrive* a verb into the headlines — "Families moving" or "He wins £2,287". But note also the tightness of the subbing. Tight, crisp subbing, with not a single wasted word, is an essential quality of all subbing. Nevertheless, in a certain kind of top it is possible for the sub to let his hair down a bit. In shorts it's the facts that matter. The short is sold on facts, and nothing else.

Take this as an example of a short gone wrong:

Dog-lover honoured

Because of his "noble, unselfish" labours in the cause of "man's best friend", Mr Lazarus Duxbury, a freelance journalist, of "Canis", Bloggs Road, Great Harwood, has been honoured by the award of a putty medal by Our Dim Friends League, an organisation which devotes its endeavours to the welfare of dogs.

Of course, every conceivable thing is wrong with this. It begins with a subsidiary clause. It has two sets of quotes and two exceptionally tired clichés in two phrases. It is written in archaic language. *It is also twice as long as it need be and that is completely damning in any short.* It is quite enough to say:

Putty-medallist

Journalist Lazarus Duxbury, of Bloggs Rd, Gt Harwood, has been awarded a putty medal by Our Dim Friends League for his work for the welfare of dogs.

Every relevant fact is there. Only the useless verbiage has gone. Room has been made for another paragraph in the story above it, or for another short to provide another interest point in the page.

Anything shorter than a short?

If a short has to be subbed tightly is there anything that has to be subbed even tighter? For those newspapers that carry nibs columns the answer if YES. "Nibs" is the usual newspaper contraction for News In Brief, though there are newspapers which call them briefs.

Here lie the half-column or more of usually headless items which are not inherently exciting but will interest somebody and can be disposed of in two, three or four lines. They have one object: to provide as many interest points as possible in as little space as possible.

I remember when I was in Glossop that I used to sit down with the council minutes and a gentleman who shall remain nameless (because he's still there) and extract from them 48 nibs on the lines of

New public lavatory is to be built in Glossop,

and

Red Cross flag day will be held in Glossop on November 23.

These were solemnly sent to the *Manchester Evening News* and the now defunct (or incorporated) Manchester *Evening Chronicle* at the rate of two a day during the month that followed. The fact that they appeared in the nibs columns of both newspapers with monotonous regularity, thereby earning Anon and I a useful income, I attribute entirely to their brevity and to the fact that they didn't *need* subbing.

For brevity is not only the Soul of Wit: it is also the soul of every nib. Not only must every surplus word be pruned out, but even non-surplus words must go in the sacred cause of squeezing as many nibs in as possible. The **BAD NIB** says:

Councillor Ephraim Threadneedle, JP, Chairman of the Barnhome urban district council, opened a swimming bath which cost £76,000 at Barnhome yesterday.

The **GOOD NIB** says:

Council chairman Ephraim Threadneedle opened a £76,000 swimming bath at Barnhome.

Or even, if it's only just in the circulation area:

£76,000 swimming bath was opened at Barnhome.

The second example will double the number of nibs; the third treble them. And the moral of that is that it's never a hack job to sub the nibs. I once got double pay for a stint on the *Sunday Express* in Manchester because in one bound I increased the number of nibs by half. It could happen to you sometime.

Note these — and beware

These are certain things a sub-editor needs to watch for in copy, lest he make the newspaper look silly. In no particular order of importance they are these:

31

1. Stories which appear to be loaded. This can cover those which are heavily-angled, one-sided, or markedly opinionated.

2. Stories which are too involved emotionally with the participants.

3. Any kind of ambiguity, particularly if it could be called a double-meaning in the sexual sense.

4. Registered trade names.

5. Any phrase which implies a record.

LOADED STORIES do neither the sub nor the newspaper any good at all, unless the paper happens to be a political tract like the *Morning Star*. In this case it's expected, and a source of comfort to the faithful and amusement to the rest. It's highly unlikely that a sub or any straight newspaper, whatever, its political leaning, would begin a story:

The Prime Minister's vicious anti-working class policies . . .

Or even:

The unchallenged genius of the miners' leader was confirmed last night by a speech he made . . .

Intros like those are clearly too loaded to get by. But less obvious ones creep in at times. It is one thing to say:

The Prime Minister was booed last night when he tried to explain a bank chief's statement on unemployment. Hecklers accused him of being devious and dishonest.

These are statements of fact. But suppose the word *justify* is used instead of *explain*. There enters then an implication that a bank chief's remarks *need* justifying. The newspaper may well take his view, and say so elsewhere, but to say so by implication in a news story will cast doubt on the balance of the rest of the report. If the story had begun:

The Prime Minister ducked and dodged questions about a bank chief last night . . .

the newspaper view would shine through the news.

It is important to emphasise that I am here concerned with straight stories, and not the work of specialist writers who are producing a kind of "hybrid" which is neither the bare news nor yet opinion, but expresses a personalised view. The Parliamentary sketch writer is entitled to say:

It was a virtuoso performance: the Prime Minister dancing and ducking, comforting the right, handing out crumbs to the left, and in the end no more quite knowing what he meant, if anything.

That was the scene as the sketch writer saw it. His name is in lights on the story. His view can be accepted or rejected. Nobody would ever be misled into thinking that it was a straight report.

Similarly a man sent to cover a by-election, or for that matter the Lord Mayor's Show, is entitled to express a personal view. But there is a difference between this and definitely loading, which means plonking yourself firmly on one side and distorting to get your effect.

I remember during the great coal crisis in the late '40s, when factories were stopping, people were sitting by empty grates, and unemployment was soaring, one newspaper explained it all away with the simple banner:

BOOMING BRITAIN BEATS THE PITS

Well, as the prophet said, if you believe that you can believe anything. Of course, people don't believe, and the disbelief rubs off on everything else. The paper concerned was later sentenced to death. Everybody else knew the gun was loaded.

Just as the sub needs to watch for this kind of angling, so he needs to take a firm line on stories which only give one side of the question. If he lets them through, the newspaper will be in danger of letters of complaint, threats of litigation, and sermons from the Press Council.

I read a story from a local correspondent which began on these lines:
Mrs Emily Dogood, 63, lives on an estate of old people's bungalows, and gets £10 a week from the council for acting as welfare worker. Last week she got a £2 rise — and immediately the council raised her rent £2.

Scandal! Parsimonious council gives with one hand and takes with the other! It seemed a fine story on the surface, but investigation produced these facts:

The rise had been granted as part of a general review of wages.

The rent had been raised as part of a general review of rents, based on the income of the tenant. The tenant of this bungalow was *Mr* Dogood, who was seven years younger than his wife, and picking up a nice pay packet.

There was absolutely no connection between the two events. *Mrs* Dogood had not had *her* rent raised because she was not a tenant. *Mr* Dogood had *his* raised along with vast numbers of other people because of the money he was earning. If the story had been printed in the original form the council would have had a justified moan, and every member of it would have felt a grudge against newspapers in general.

Subs, like reporters, need to remember that there's usually another side, and it needs to be chased out. If the other side is represented by a cautious chap saying "No comment", then the executives, perhaps with legal advice will have to decide whether to go ahead anyway. If they do then great caution will be needed to ensure that nothing about which there is the slightest doubt is given as a fact, but is always attributed to whoever is making the allegation. Only rarely can a "no-comment" story safely begin:

Accountant Charles Grudge has been ordered to pull down his new £25,000 house because his kitchen is one foot longer than was shown on the plans.

It usually has to be:

Accountant Charles Grudge said yesterday that the council had ordered him to pull down is new £25,000 house because his kitchen is one foot longer than shown on the plans. Last night the Town Clerk refused to comment.

The reason for this is that later on it may turn out that the council had all sorts of other reasons, possibly equally idiotic, for making the order. The house may also have been built 30 feet away from the agreed spot and right over the footpath to the local comprehensive school; it may have been faced with red, white and blue tiles, thereby ruining the appearance of the fourth loveliest village in England; or Mr Grudge may be an eccentric who instead of installing proper sanitation has built a solitary privy slap between his front gate and a public telephone call box.

The original story may well turn out to be not only the truth but also the whole truth. Nevertheless, unless the sub *knows* it to be the whole truth because of independent evidence he must treat allegations as allegations, and not as facts.

EMOTIONAL INVOLVEMENT on the part of a reporter can bring its dangers, and a sub needs to watch for signs of it. It can lead to the kind of errors dealt with in the section on loaded stories above — political bias or an over-readiness to accept a sob-story as its face value.

But it also comes out in another way — the urge to fill the story with over-emotive phrases. We have the grief-stricken widow, eyes welling with tears; the train crash angled on the child's doll in the wreckage; the beauty, diligence, honesty and unparalleled mental powers of the Ghanaian immigrant who can only get a job sweeping up dog-ends dropped by cheap white trash. If the copy seems *emotionally* angled, the sub should suspect it. That is not to say that if some executive decides that Page Five will be devoted to the Tear-Jerker of the Month he should do his best to take the tears out of it. But by and large he should bear in mind that what is demanded of him is, in the old phrase, a plain tale well told.

AMBIGUITY is an ever-present danger, particularly if one of the meanings is a dirty one.

Certain words need watching because people are forever applying double meanings to them. Some words are practically impossible to use in the plural: I can recall half a dozen occasions when the most awful ambiguities got into print on that alone.

One of the finest I've seen lately (exact, unamended quote):

A BLACK medicine man who allegedly cut off a 10-year-old boy's tongue and genital organs, appeared in the Randfontein Magistrates' Court yesterday on a charge of attempted murder. . .

A hospital spokesman said yesterday the boy was "holding his own".

It is also important to watch for words that change in meaning. *Pot,* for example, formerly needed watching because it was read as chamber pot; now care is necessary because it is a synonym for cannabis.

TRADE NAMES cause a lot of trouble because if one particular product becomes established its name tends to be used to cover a whole range of products. It then gets in the paper as a generic term — "She sat there drinking coke* and playing with the zipp* on her liberty bodice*" — and immediately the manufacturers slap in a letter of complaint. I've known them get an apologetic paragraph in when the infringement has happened more than once.

In *Doing it in style* I gave a comprehensive list of the dangerous trade names. Here I confine myself to some of the most common ones, with alternative words or phrases. The important thing to remember is that if you use a trade name it *must* have an initial cap and you *must* be sure you're on the right product. If you say that the girl mentioned above was strangled by her liberty bodice and it turns out to be a similar but dangerous bit of clobber imported from Hong Kong, then you're really in trouble.

Trade name	Alternative
Aspro	aspirin
Biro	ball-pen
Breathalyzer	breath tester
BriNylon	nylon
Carricot	carry-cot
Catseye	road stud
Cellophane	transparent wrapping
Coalite	smokeless fuel
Coke (Coca-Cola)	cola
Elastoplast	sticking plaster
Fibreglass	glass fibre
Hoover	vacuum cleaner
Jeep	Use it, if you're sure it's not a Land Rover
Photostat	photo-copy
Plasticine	modelling copy
Primus-stove	pressure-stove
Rediffusion	relay-radio or TV
Sellotape	sticky tape
Spam	luncheon meat
Technicolor	colour
Terylene	artificial fibre
Thermos	vacuum flask
Vaseline	petroleum jelly

*Three trade names. That's how easy it is.

One oddity that doesn't strictly belong with the trade names: Spiritualism must always have a cap S or the letters of complaint will flow in. This is because it's officially registered as a religion.

RECORDS are dangerous things. I don't mean records in the sense of gigantic long jumps, or phenomenal achievements in the Pork Pie Eating Championship at Birchington Carnival. I mean stories in which people lay claim to something on which it's virtually impossible to check. Only a national newspaper sub who has let through a story beginning

The oldest Boer War veteran . . .

can fully realise just how many of them there are. Even at this stage there must be more oldest Boer War veterans than there were final farewell tours by the Chocolate Coloured Coon.

Any phrase like this seems to bring out the worst in readers of the I-don't-expect-to-read-anything-correct-in-newspapers-so-I-wasn't-surprised variety. The only possible rule for the sub is this: IF THERE'S A SUPERLATIVE IN IT, TREAT IT WITH SUSPICION. If you CAN'T CHECK IT, MODIFY IT. Beware of all stories which begin

The oldest man in Derbyshire . . .
Britain's smallest steeplejack . . .
The first Englishman to visit the South Pole since . . .
The only woman missionary to . . .
The biggest fish ever caught in . . .
The last teenager to pilot a Spitfire . . .
The last man to see quiet, home-loving Sandra Higgs alive . . .

With claims like these, let someone else make them, not the newspaper. Unless, of course, you can find it in the Guinness of Book of Records.

Who did you say was speaking?

One of the most difficult jobs for a sub to handle is the reporting of speeches and occasionally interviews. If he is faced with a colour piece from an established writer he has no problems. But suppose he is given 20 paragraphs of news agency copy on a speech and asked for 6-7 inches of single column?

The first rule is this: **NEVER BEGIN WITH A QUOTE.** The reason is simple: It's only when you know who is talking that you can assess the value of the quote. In many cases the quote only becomes intelligible after you know the name of the speaker. Look at his example:

"I am in favour of ending all censorship of films said . . .

The key phrase is going to follow the word *said*. Until the reader knows *who* said it the quote has no value. If it was uttered by the publisher of a soft-porn magazine, then who cares? If, on the other hand the speaker was the founder Chairman of IIMBI (If it moves, Ban It) — well, we've got a story. And the reader ought not to have to wait till the second clause to find out that it exists. He should have it simply served up:

Sir Cyril Moralist, who for years has denounced all forms of pornography, said yesterday that he was now IN FAVOUR of ending censorship of films.

The quote-first practice becomes much worse when it's a very long one. The intro that follows is taken, only slightly amended, from a local newspaper, reporting not a speech but an interview:

"My personal opinion is that the ban on overtime has not proved to be as effective as they had hoped, and as a consequence they are taking this action against the inspectors to aggravate the position still further" said Ald John Thomas, JP, Chairman of the Transport Committee, to the "Advertiser", commenting on the strike by local busmen.

Leaving aside the mixture of gobbledygook and pomposity of the quote (which no newspaper should allow unless it's consciously taking the mickey) and the fact that the story was set hanging indent (which quote marks throw out of balance), this is not so much an intro but more an obstacle race. It raises these questions to halt the reader in his tracks as he wades through:

> *Whose* personal opinion?
> *What* ban on overtime?
> As effective as *who* hoped?
> *What* action against the inspectors?
> Aggravate *what* position?

Only in the last phrase is there an indication what the story is about — a bus strike. Now I am well aware that the readers would know that there was a bus strike on, but that is no reason for the local newspaper to make their lives even more difficult. It could have said simply:

Alderman John Thomas, transport committee chairman, said yesterday that local busmen had gone on strike because their overtime ban had not been as effective as they had hoped.

The number of words has been cut by more than half, from 58 to 28, without losing anything the reader needs to know. More important, the facts are in logical sequence, with every new one dependent on something that has gone before, not on something that follows further down the story. Thus it fulfils the requirements not merely for a report of a speech or interview, but for a report of anything.

With this obstacle out of the way, it is possible to consider ways of handling the speech. The first thing to do is: **DECIDE WHAT SORT OF SPEECH IT IS.** For speeches fall largely into two classes.

1. News speeches, which provide some item of news which at any rate will provide a straight intro.

2. Speech speeches, which just provide a lot of talk, in most cases a lot of boring old twaddle. (The phrase speech speeches is freely adapted from the words of Shirley Temple Black, who divides the world into politician people, writer people and so on, and *people people*.)

NEWS SPEECHES are easy. You just find the news point and peg the story on it. In most cases the news is far more interesting than the views. This applies not merely to the big-time stuff, to the chap who sits down with shaking pen to write:

A 200-megaton bomb will be dropped on Moscow at noon on Tuesday unless the Russians release a jailed businessman.

The Prime Minister announced this last night . . .

It applies equally to the sub who wades through the platitudes uttered or muttered at the annual dinner of Stoney Middleton Rotary Club and produces the intro:

Mr Charles Strongi'th'arm is retiring after 57 years as secretary of Stoney Middleton Rotary Club — "to allow more time for other activities" he told members on Wednesday.

Far too often local newspapers expect readers to climb over half a dozen pars of phrase-making by some ancient worthy before coming to some newsy item. Get a JP talking to the Women's Institute about his work, and there half-way down will be an undistinguished paragraph which says:

"We as magistrates have met together and decided unanimously that the only way to deal with outbreaks of soccer hooliganism is to increase the sentences on the hooligans to the very limit of our statutory powers" he went on.

That par contains news. It's the job of the sub, faced with the failure of the reporter to do his own work properly, to turn that speech into a news story.

Soccer hooligans at Calver Sough now face maximum sentences when they appear in court. The new tough line was decided by the magistrates when . . .

If there is a news point in a speech the reporter should have found it. But if he's failed, then the sub must turn it round for him.

SPEECH SPEECHES are much more difficult. There are few people who make a speech speech worthy of putting on record.

Politicians are prone to moan that their jewelled phrases never get into print. The readers, I suspect, would rise in revolt against the newspaper which took its cue from its ancestors and published large slabs of dull and dreary political argument, mostly culled from speakers' handbooks, all of which has been said before.

Ministers of religion would no doubt like their sermons published in full in their local papers, but no good would be served by doing so. The faithful have already heard The Word, and in some cases the same Word every Sunday for years. Faced with such tracts, the Unrighteous — that is the nine-tenths of the population who rarely go to church — would vent their wrath not on the parson but on the newspaper.

What neither the Church nor the State realises is that it is surprisingly easy to get any *original* thought into the papers, and here lies the first clue to the presentation of speeches: **HAS THE SPEAKER SAID ANYTHING UNEXPECTED OR PROVOCATIVE OR DISTURBING OR ORIGINAL?**

If he has just trotted out all the old clichés, and said all the things he might have been expected to say, is it worth recording? To demonstrate the point by going to extremes, a story which begins

The Bishop of London said yesterday that he firmly believed in the existence of God

is not a story at all, and the reader must be forgiven if he stops short at the first paragraph and moves on to a totally-unexpected tale about an abortion racket at a posh girls' boarding school. Even these days what would you expect the bishop to say anyway? It is only when the sub can write

The Bishop of London said yesterday that he had ceased to believe in God

that he is really in business. Similarly, if a far-left MP expresses *doubts* about nationalisation that's news; if he says he favours it, then why should a newspaper mention it? If a Catholic priest says he likes his pint that's no surprise because we rather expect it; but if a Methodist minister says it, that's news because he breaking out and a lot of people are going to be upset by it. Here comes the **UNEXPECTED** element, and this is the most valuable of all from a newspaper point of view.

The **PROVOCATIVE** statement also has its virtues, and can produce many a good intro. It can be found where someone is challenging any preconceived idea or plan. It can be found at national level, perhaps in some statement by that well-known religious figure who almost daily misses the most excellent opportunities of keeping his mouth shut:

The Archbishop said yesterday that Britain should think seriously about whether it wishes to make criminals out of young people who took "soft" drugs.*

It can also be found at local level, in stories that make the local newspaper but never get beyond it:

Alderman Josiah Stranahan advocated banning all unmarried expectant mothers from public baths in Abney, on the grounds that they might corrupt teenagers, when he addressed St George's Young Wives on Tuesday.

---

*OK, he's not said it yet — but who'll take a bet that he won't tomorrow?

This is the kind of point that rouses emotions — people furiously agree or furiously disagree. To seize on it is a good way of reporting a speech.

The **DISTURBING** intro has its virtues too. If you can't excite or stimulate people there's no harm in making their flesh creep, providing you don't do it too often:

Britain will have race riots worse than any yet experienced in the United States unless there is a complete ban on immigration, a Tory leader warned yesterday.

(I *know* that this is slightly cart-before-horse if one strictly interprets the rules outlined above, but there are exceptions to all rules. In this case the first statement has a certain drama, it does not confuse the reader with a mysterious "I", and it can all be absorbed at one glance. Compare its ease of reading with: "*I am convinced that if the present rate of immigration is allowed to continue then we shall face race riots worse than any yet experienced in the United States*", *said a Tory leader yesterday.*)

Likewise, at the local paper level:

A doctor warned yesterday that typhoid could kill half the children in Dinting unless something was done about the state of public lavatories in Howard Road.

Finally, was anything **ORIGINAL** said? This is the last hope, because it is so rare. With few exceptions, who in public life, says anything original these days? Nonetheless, it is as well to keep an eye open for original thoughts. They are so rare as to be worthwhile.

These points to look for are not the whole story when it comes to subbing a speech. There remains the question: **WHAT ELSE HAPPENED AT THE MEETING?** And this can sometimes provide the best angle to a story. I once remember reading with a sort of horrified fascination an account of the mouthings of a parliamentary candidate. Not one word he uttered could have been of the slightest interest to more than a quarter of one per cent of the readership. But the last paragraph reported that there was a scuffle during the speech and the speaker was hit by an egg, and later enquiries established that it was one hell of a meeting. I said at the time that I could only recall one comparable incident, and that was when a freelance photographer of my acquaintance was dispatched to get a photograph of the mayor presenting prizes at a swimming gala and came back empty-handed because His Worship had fallen into the bath.

But there are all sorts of incidents short of egg-throwing which can be used to bring the report of a meeting to life. Heckling for a start — there are few things more lively than a good exchange between a speaker and a persistent member of the audience. The speaker losing his temper is a good bet, and that happens astonishingly often. The solid block of "planted" opposition often provides a good angle.

Further points to note:

BEWARE of reported speech, especially in intros. It can lead to confusion about the exact meaning:

Father Grazier was the best vicar St George's ever had, said Mrs Mary Backward at the parish meeting last week.

Is he no longer? Is he dead? Is Mrs Backward referring to some vicar in the past and knocking the present vicar? The sentence is grammatically correct, but the meaning becomes much more clear *and instantly recognisable* if the dramatic present is used:

Father Grazier is the best vicar St George's has ever had, said . . .

BEWARE of mixing up two speakers by beginning an account of the second with a quote. This can be counted on to baffle any reader:

"I am strongly in favour of a complete ban on further immigration" he added.

"Anyone who is in favour of such a policy is a reactionary Fascist racialist" said the next speaker, Mrs Joanna Pauker.

In this case the reader is entitled to wonder if the first speaker has had a brainstorm. In the other it is merely a matter of a non sequitur. In most it is just a question of making it easier for the reader.

AVOID continually adding phrases like "he added", and "he vouch-safed" at the end of quotes. Apart from that great old maxim THERE ARE FEW BETTER WORDS THAN SAID it is generally much better to have a straight sequence of unbroken quotes. Here the device of starting and ending a long extract with outsize quote marks, thus disposing of a vast number of inverted commas, is a useful one.

TRY, in a long speech, to break it up into sections, possibly by subject matter:

Mr Silverwoman listed the enormous achievements of the present Parliament:

THE DEATH PENALTY, a relic of the barbarous past, had finally been abolished, and the community was no longer stained with the taint of taking human life . . .

ABORTION had been legalised, thus ensuring that no more unwanted children would be brought into the world . . .

HOMOSEXUALITY was legal in private, and any man could now covet his neighbour's husband without transgressing the law . . .

CENSORSHIP of plays by the Lord Chamberlain had ended and it was now possible . . .

The eye is carried through by the key words instead of boggling at a solid slab of type.

Bill posters will be popular

There is an extra job which falls to subs in most office: the writing of bills. Here I offer three bits of advice:

1. DON'T FORGET THEM. The chief sub, who will be under pressure from the circulation manager, will get weary if every time he checks whether you've done a bill he gets the answer "No". If subs in your office are called upon to write bills, write them, and don't leave the job to someone else.

2. MAKE THEM TEASING. The function of a bill is not to tell the whole story. If it does that people may decide it's not worth buying the paper. Always leave a question unanswered, Suppose, for example, you have a Rolling Stone arrested on a drugs charge. It is as well not to give all this information on the bill. "Rolling Stone" must not be dropped as these are the emotive words. So the bill can read:

ROLLING STONE ARRESTED

"What for?" the customers will cry, rushing for their paper.

If, however, the pop "star" is a member of the Nadgers, a group hitherto unknown outside Rawtenstall, it is better to disguise the fact and concentrate on the pulling aspect of the drugs charge. The situation is reversed:

POP STAR ON DRUGS CHARGE

"Which one?" the customers will ask.

When the Stone case is over, the bill should read

ROLLING STONE CASE RESULT

and *not*

ROLLING STONE FINED

which gives too much away. But when the mini-star goes down, the sentence can be used as a tempter:

POP STAR GETS SIX MONTHS

This way there is always something left for the reader to pay his money for:

3. WRITE A LOT OF THEM. Many stories contain a number of bills waiting to be dug out. A national newspaper dealing with a demand for a salary of £150 a week by students at the London School of Economics does not merely have a London bill on its hands:

LONDON STUDENTS' PAY DEMAND

It can also scatter bills round universities and colleges all over the country:

£150 SALARY FOR STUDENTS URGED

It can find out where the activists come from and bill accordingly:

ACCRINGTON STUDENT IN PAY RUMPUS
BACUP STUDENT IN PAY RUMPUS

It then only needs some MP or bishop to make noises in support and more local bills can say:

RAMSBOTTOM MP IN STUDENT SHOCK
HASLINGDEN BISHOP IN STUDENT SHOCK

Good bills sell newspapers. It's worth while giving them a bit of care.

Remember the people in the back streets of Derby

THE words above are those of Arthur Christiansen, for 25 years editor of the *Daily Express*. He reiterated them time and time again, driving home to reporters and especially to subs that their main audience did not consist of highbrows and intellectuals, capable of unravelling for themselves complex stories on complex subjects written in a complex way. In one bulletin to staff he wrote:

It would do everyone connected with Fleet Street (especially editors) a power of good if they spent an occasional day off in unfamiliar territory seeing the newspaper reader as he is at work and play. In familiar territory in the neighbourhood of your own home you don't get the same perspective.

I journeyed from Rhyl to Prestatyn on Sunday past lines of boarding houses, caravans, wooden huts, shacks, tents, and heaven knows what else. In every one of them there were newspaper readers. Happy citizens, worthy, fine people, but not in the least like the reader Fleet Street seems to be writing for.

These people are not interested in Glyndebourne or vintage claret or opera or the Sitwells or dry-as-dust economics or tough politics. It is our job to interest them in everything. It requires the highest degree of skill and ingenuity.

The last two sentences contain the germ of the whole thing. The complete newspaper must cover the whole range of human affairs, and some of them are extremely dull. In the final analysis it is the job of the sub to catch the reader's interest, and by direct and simple writing keep it all the way through. Christiansen was talking about Fleet Street, but the lesson applies with equal force to local papers.

To achieve this simplicity and readability calls for a clear orderly mind on the part of the sub. But there are certain rules which, if followed, will contribute to it. In this chapter I have set them out under separate headings.

Short and sweet

Always remember that a short sentence is an easy sentence. From a newspaper point of view the full stop is the greatest single aid to clarity and readability. I do not suggest that all stories should read like parodies of one of Lord Beaverbrook's more stirring leaders:

Churchill speaks. But will the nation listen? Indeed it will. For why? Because it is sound at heart. Its will remains strong.

But over-long sentences are death to readability. They are usually of involved construction, and involved sentences have to be read twice to get their full meaning. It is an absolute truth for subs to say: **NOTHING THAT CAN'T BE ABSORBED AT FIRST READING OUGHT TO APPEAR IN A NEWSPAPER.** Yet night after night and week after week these jigsaw puzzles get into print.

Take the following example. To avoid distortion it was selected from one batch of copy, and many worse cases occur. It is the second paragraph of a story. The first tells how a Mr William Bowering's greenhouse plants died after someone put weedkiller in his water tank. It goes on:—

Stated to have been living at the time in a caravan on adjoining land owned by Mr Bowering, Edward Thomas Street, 32, a building sub-contractor, now living at Manor Road, Enfield, was found guilty by a jury yesterday of maliciously damaging the boxes in which the plants were kept and the staging on which they rested to a value of £150.

Let us analyse this entence in terms of readability and consider the obstacles the reader has to surmount.

Stated to have been living at the time in a caravan . . .

WHO stated that WHO was living in a caravan at WHAT time?

on adjoining land . . .

Land adjoining WHAT?

owned by Mr Bowering, Edward Thomas Street, 32, a building sub-contractor . . .

Note the unhappy juxtaposition of the two names

was found guilty by a jury yesterday of maliciously damaging the boxes . . .

We have to wait for the rest of the sentence to find how "the boxes" came into it.

But apart from these points there is the simple, overriding one: It's just too much of a mouthful. Split it up and it becomes intelligible:

The man responsible was Edward Street, a 32-year-old building sub-contractor who used to live in a caravan on adjoining land owned by Mr Bowering.

Street, now of Manor Road, Enfield, was found guilty of maliciously damaging £150-worth of boxes and staging affected by the weedkiller.

I am not saying that this is the best way to do it, because in fact the whole story needs recasting. I merely make the point that one complicated sentence has been made more readable by converting it into two, and the number of words reduced in the process.

This simple subbing operation becomes even more important when the sentence contains what amounts to a list of things. My mind boggled when I read this in a local paper:

> The busmen nationally are claiming a minimum wage of £150 per week, a standard week of five scheduled daily duties of eight hours each day with two rest days, also time and a half rate on rest days based on a guaranteed day of eight hours, improved spread-over duties, holidays increased from 10 days to 14 days with pay, one-man operation drivers to be paid an additonal 40 per cent of the normal rate of pay, and to discuss the penal clause (lightning strikes, etc.).

Here is a case where the reader must be helped along by good verbal and optical breaks:

> The busmen nationally are claiming:
>
> 1 A minimum £150 a week for five scheduled eight-hour duties, with two rest days.
>
> 2 Time-and-a-half for rest-day work, based on a guaranteed eight hours, with improved spread-over duties.
>
> 3 Forty pence in the £ over normal rates for drivers on one-man buses.
>
> 4 Talks on the penal clause covering such things as lightning strikes.
>
> 5 Fourteen days' paid holiday instead of ten.

Breaking one sentence into SIX and setting them out gives the customer a much better chance of understanding a rather complex situation. Note, incidentally, that the sequence has been changed so that the shortest point comes last, thereby avoiding the running together of two drop figures. In the process of rewriting the jargon phrases and the superfluous words have disappeared.

Always remember that if a reader can't absorb a sentence at first go he is likely to rapidly move elsewhere — either to another story, or to another newspaper, which is worse.

Subject, verb, object

It is a good thing to remember that the simplest construction is usually the best, and particularly that an active voice is usually better than a passive one. *The cat sat on the mat* is easier to comprehend than *The mat was being sat on by the cat*. It is also much shorter, and that is a virtue.

Yet many writers go out of their way to construct sentences which from a sense point of view run backwards, presumably because they have become bored with straightforward writing:

Mr John Goldfinger was attacked by the Clerk of Works for . . . rather than

The Clerk of Works attacked Mr John Goldfinger for . . .

Or

The Ghanaian team was beaten by Britain

rather than

Britain beat the Ghanaian team.

But even worse is the use of the passive combined with laboured inversions:

Attacked for his part in the programme was Mr John Goldfinger . . .

What two members of the art department were told by Tower Bridge magistrates . . .

How they finally escaped was related by Miss Annie Crackling . . .

The inverted sentence is banned by some newspapers. This is, perhaps, carrying the rule book a bit far. But it is a device to be used with caution.

Another distortion to beware of is the practice of beginning sentences with participles and subsidiary clauses. It is a form of writing that is difficult to absorb because the subsidiary clause usually doesn't make any sense till the reader has reached the main clause. The reader is therefore slowed down and frequently has to back-track to get the full meaning.

The greenhouse story, which I quoted from earlier as an example of an over-long sentence, also had the demerit of beginning with a participle and a subsidiary clause. Here is another, in which two successive sentences have the same fault:

Pleading guilty to unauthorised possession of cannabis resin and a form of LSD found when detectives raided his room in Gertrude Street, Chelsea, John James Cable, 23, a chef, who was formerly saxophonist and road manager of the Nashville Teens pop group, was remanded for a fortnight for medical reports.

Found asleep on a mattress in the room, an attractive blonde German girl Rosita Wagener, 20, of the same address, also pleaded guilty to the charges and was similarly remanded.

Note the obstacles the reader has to surmount on his way through. These are the questions that are raised in his mind as he plods on — questions that are only answered further on:

WHO pleaded guilty?

WHOSE room?

WHO was asleep?

Three questions, and three too many. They are a burden the reader is spared if a simple construction is used:

John Cable, former member of the Nashville Teens pop group and now a chef, admitted having cannabis resin and LSD. The drugs were found when detectives raided his room in Gertrude Street, Chelsea.

Blonde Rosita Wagener, a 20-year-old German who was asleep on a mattress when the police arrived, also pleaded guilty. She and Cable, 23, were remanded for medical reports.

The number of words has been reduced. But, more important, the story has gained in clarity by the simple construction of the sentences.

Another danger lies in wait for those who begin sentences with subsidiary clauses: that of confusing the reader with pronouns. It becomes easy for the addict to slip in a pronoun which refers to a noun still to be identified.

Although he was a gin drinker, Mr Trebor Ross always asked for half pints of bitter to spare his friends expense . . .

Despite his success as a sub-editor, Mr Donald Yo Ung decided to go back on the road . . .

In view of his strong feelings about cleanliness, Mr Cuthbert Geoffrey launched a Change Underwear Twice A Day campaign . . .

In each of these cases, the reader has to absorb the second clause before the first acquires any meaning. If this kind of construction is used the noun must always come before the pronoun:

Although Mr Trebor Ross was a gin drinker, he always asked for half pints of bitter to spare his friends expense . . .

But far better to decide which is the main clause and put it first. Either:

Mr Trebor Ross was a gin drinker, but he always asked for half pints of bitter to spare his friends expense . . .

or:

Mr Trebor Ross always asked for half pints of bitter to save his friends expense, although he was a gin drinker . . .

This way the reader starts at the beginning and gratefully carries on.

If it defines, no commas

One popular way of confusing the reader is by the over-liberal use of commas. The rule is: ONLY USE A COMMA WHERE THERE WOULD BE A VERBAL PAUSE.

The most common misuse of commas in newspapers — and here the sub is to blame, because if he didn't put them in he should have taken them out — is in barricading off defining clauses. It is essential to understand the difference between a defining clause and a descriptive clause. The first contributes vital information, and the second merely adds information. There are two rough-and-ready ways of testing:

1. If it can be left out without damage it's a *descriptive clause;* if it can't it's a *defining clause.*

2. If it is read aloud without pause it's a *defining clause;* if it can't be it's a *descriptive clause.*

Now this is not infallible, but it works so many times it doesn't matter. Take this sentence:

The man who ate 408 pork pies at Birchington Carnival died in hospital last night, three hours after his stomach exploded with a roar heard in Margate.

The words *who ate 408 pork pies at Birchington Carnival* are vital to the sense. There is no verbal pause after *man* or after *Carnival.* The words define the man we are talking about. But if we say:

Mr Kenilworth ("Elastic Guts") Blown, who ate 408 pork pies at Birchington Carnival, died in hospital . . .

the same clause becomes a descriptive one. The anonymous "the man" is replaced by a clearly-defined chap — Mr Kenilworth ("Elastic Guts") Blown.

Whether the clause is descriptive or defining can depend on its position in the story, and whether the person or thing has been previously identified. This sentence begins a story:

The eel-and-pie restaurant that burst into flames on Sunday night had been raided by police a fortnight earlier.

In this case the clause "that burst into flames on Sunday night" defines which eel-and-pie restaurant we're talking about and runs right through without commas. But if the story says:

Two men arrested outside Joe's Caff in Camberwell Old Road were accused of arson last night.

The eel-and-pie restaurant, which burst into flames on Sunday night, had been raided by police a fortnight earlier

the clause "which burst into flames on Sunday night" is a descriptive clause. We already know which caff we're talking about. It is therefore divided by commas from the rest of the sentence.

This odd use of commas also crops up in newspapers which latch on to the *Times*-style practice of using a defining phrase in front of a man's name:

Premier Margaret Gandhi shouted . . .

Opposition Leader Neil O'Scargill replied . . .
Drug-addict Rolph Treacle died . . .
Colonel's daughter Angela Bloodnut married . . .

Whether the phrases are regarded as titular (Premier) or descriptive (drug-addict) they should not be followed by commas. Neither should the names, which define which Premier or drug-addict we are talking about. We should not, after all, say:

Field-Marshal, Harold Wilson, attacked . . .

much as he'd like it, or for that matter:

Bearded, Rolph Treacle, died . . .

There is no more justification for putting commas here than in the earlier examples.

Fewer words, better sense

SOME newspapers suffer from superfluous words in the same way that some women suffer from superfluous hair. There is an easy remedy for the first, and it's known as a good sub. He can shoot through a piece of copy and without doing any rewriting strike out every word which is not performing a useful function. This is the key: **IF IT'S NOT DOING A JOB, KNOCK IT OUT.** Each word in a newspaper must earn its space.

Here is a sentence from a councillor's speech which leapt out at me from a local weekly:

Members of the public should be given the opportunity of examining the proposition more closely in order to get a better understanding of the complicated problems involved.

Merely by straight subbing on copy this can be made to read:

People should have a chance to examine the proposal more closely, so that they understand what a complicated problem it is.

The number of words has been reduced by a fifth, and the sentence is more readable for it.

In the next example the words in roman could have been removed completely.

Mr Colquohon said that it had to be admitted that *Wilson's appearance was intimidating, but that* in itself *did not mean* that *an offence had been committed. After Wilson had been found guilty* by the magistrates, *Mr Colquohon asked the magistrates to deal leniently with him, and said* that a reading of *the probation officer's report indicated* that there had been *an improvement in his behaviour* since the early part of *this year.*

The whole paragraph could clearly have benefited by rewriting completely. But it is improved by a simple process of striking out 25 words. If a sub can do no more, he can do that.

These superfluous words creep up on newspapers in several forms, and the sub must guard against them all.

There is the unnecessary use of THAT, which can be seen in the last example above.

There are the QUALIFYING WORDS, which in so far as they qualify at all are ridiculous — the true facts (facts *are* true by definition), the well-known pop singer (the description is either unnecessary or untrue).

There are the AUTOMATIC WORDS, which prefix nouns out of habit, in the way that nobody ever has a cold, but always a bad cold. Note these examples, where the words in roman have just got there:

It meant an end to his cherished *belief that he could appeal to the consensus rather than the party.*

She had considerable *difficulty in holding her skirt down.*

He chose the psychological *moment to attack.*

He expressed his grateful *thanks to the reporters.*

He said there was a serious *danger of foot-and-mouth disease spreading over the whole country.*

She broke all-time *records with her low-cut dress.*

There are the straight cases of TAUTOLOGY, beloved of our rulers, in which two words are made to do the work of one:

broad daylight	*more preferable*
completely untrue	*prejudged in advance*
continue to remain	*together with*
definite decisions	*weather conditions*

Then there is the most pernicious form of all — the dreadful circumlocutions, the words that just seem to creep in. Note these examples, and their simple substitutes:

acted as	*was*
adjacent to	*near*
as a result of	*because*
as from	*from*
as of this moment	*now*
at an early date	*soon*
at present	*now*
at the present time	*now*
at this moment in time	*now*
conspicuous by their absence	*not present*
despite the fact that	*although*
during the course of	*during*
effect a saving	*save*
filled to capacity	*full*

give consideration to	*consider*
in attendance	*present*
leaving much to be desired	*is unsatisfactory*
preparatory to	*before*

The list could go on *ad nauseam*. In some newspapers, unfortunately, it does.

What do you mean, PRETTY?

The dangers of calling a woman attractive or beautiful should by now be self-evident. Sometimes she is, beyond dispute, but more often adjectives like this raise a good old laugh among friends as well as enemies — and, more important, among readers if a picture goes in, too.

Yet this is not the most serious aspect of the thing from a sub's point of view, which is that many reporters drop in adjectives out of habit. This is not merely a question of the psychological moments and the considerable difficulties mentioned in the last section. It seems rather to be a feeling that a noun on its own is somehow naked and ought not to be allowed out in the world without an adjective to cover its shame.

Thus we have the *neat* semi-detached council house, and I feel some reporters would make it so even if it were like a pig-sty. There is also the trade-union leader who will stay *burly* even after a diet has reduced his weight to 10 stone; the cinema which is automatically *luxury* even though hooligans have turned it into a scene of squalor; the express train that is inevitably *crack* although it takes longer on the journey than it did in Queen Victoria's day.

This is not an argument against adjectives, but only against the kind of adjective which is just so much useless clutter. Indeed, I am inclined to think that the reaction against adjectival writing has gone too far. Many subs are now *too* ready to strike out the *pink-washed* that comes before *bungalow* or the *squat, balding* that comes before *club-owner*. This kind of description, in my view, adds to the story. It gives a mental image of the article and therefore helps the reader.

The points it to confine adjectives to those that do some work, and even then to beware of over-use. This particularly applies to strings of adjectives used *Time*-style:

Handsome, grey-haired, tea-buying sub-editor T Quatermass Ross . . .

Tough, Scottish, amateur aeronaut and copy-taster Herbert Alexander Stimpson . . .

A couple of adjectives are really the limit. Anything more is too much of a mouthful.

Composite adjectives should also be approached with care for the same reason.

The four-men-and-a-dog expedition

and

The ten-men-and-two-women jury

are phrases distinguished only by their clumsiness, and can well be done without.

Look out, NUJ, it's the NPA

In these times, when official and semi-official organisations are proliferating, new sets of initials rear their ugly heads each day. Subs need to remember two facts about them:

1. Most abbreviations of this kind are meaningless to a large number of readers.

2. The use of a lot of sets of initials in a story will disfigure it visually.

There are some, perhaps a dozen, abbreviations for the names of organisations which have so passed into the language that they can be used without explanation. These include BBC, ITV, RAF, CID and GPO.

But a far, far greater number need explaining *every time they are used.* Not to do this puts too great a burden on the reader, and gives him a feeling of inadequacy which may be entirely justifiable but does the newspaper no good.

For the popular market it is simply not good enough to talk about the IMF and EFTA and the WMO and OEEC and the ATA. Any mention of the WHO and younger readers are likely to think you're talking of the pop group rather than that worthy World Health Organisation.

The rule is: **SPELL OUT FIRST, AND AFTER THAT AVOID THE ABBREVIATIONS AS MUCH AS POSSIBLE.**

This is usually quite practicable. I saw a story in which the initials NUBE appeared in every third line. It was difficult to read because the incessant NUBE NUBE NUBE leaped out of the page to the exclusion of everything else. This could have been avoided by referring to the National Union of Bank Employees at the first mention and to union ever afterwards. Similarly the Amateur Athletic Association can be called the association, and the Social Club for Expectant Au Pair Girls can be referred to not as SCFEAPG but just as the club.

There is one exception to this rule: those useful abbreviations that form words which have passed into the language, or at any rate the language of some people. Such are Unesco, Gatt and Nalgo. These can appear as normal words. But of course, apart from obvious ones like Naafi and Ernie, they must also be defined first.

Yes, but who was George Brown?

In this quest for simplicity the sub must always remember that he probably knows more about the subject than the average reader. He must therefore identify all the time, and recap on all subjects which are not absolutely fresh in the public mind.

Even names which to him register at once may well be meaningless to the reader. What is even more likely is that although the reader may feel he recognises the name he can't quite place it, and the sub must do the placing.

It must be remembered that most members of the public haven't heard of most members of the Cabinet, so each needs identifying.

Likewise, ancient film stars must be identified as such for the benefit of younger readers, and teenage pop stars for the benefit of older ones.

Don't forget, too, the need to identify for a while peers who have recently been elevated under different names.

Organisations must also be identified.

The Confederation of British Industry.
Is that an employers' outfit?

The Independent Television Authority.
Is that the body that looks after the whole lot?

The Union of Shop, Distributive and Allied Workers.
Is that the mainly-Co-op one, or am I thinking of NUDAW?

Every time a new subject comes into the news, or an old subject is revived, the reader must be put into the picture as briefly as possible. Minds need refreshing. Not only old men forget.

And my next point is . . .

One way to achieve simplicity in a complicated story is to use the old point-by-point technique. This is especially useful when it comes to reports, White Papers and similar stodge, which often require an experienced translator. The best course is usually to convert into simple English and classify and sectionalise as much as possible. Here are two ways of doing the same thing:

The report also recommends these changes:

Public Schools should be abolished and their funds distributed among cultural projects for manual workers.

The report also recommends these changes:

1 Public Schools should be abolished and their funds distributed among cultural projects for manual workers.

Parents of children at the schools should continue paying fees even after their children are transferred to state schools.

Badges bearing the word SNOB should be worn by all the transferred children as a penance.

Exams should be abolished to remove the last traces of pressure on the children in the new schools.

2 Parents of children at the schools should continue paying fees even after their children are transferred to state schools.

3 Badges bearing the word SNOB should be worn by all transferred children as a penance.

4 Exams should be abolished to remove the last traces of pressure on the children in the new schools.

This technique of setting out points can clarify an otherwise-muddy story. It can also be employed to give a sequence of events their full flavour:

At 10.15 Mrs Belcher phone the Gas Board and said she'd locked their fitter in the wash-house and wouldn't let him out till they fixed her cooker.

At 10.20 the showroom manager phone Mrs Belcher and said the police would be called unless the fitter was released. Mrs Belcher said No.

At 10.25 the district manager phoned to tell Mrs Belcher that she would be charged for all the time the fitter was detained.

At 10.45 a van arrive . . .

There are many occasions when this kind of sequence can be used effectively. There are also many on which the old question and answer technique can put shape into an otherewise formless tale. This is at its most effective reporting cross-examination in court cases, but it can also be employed with press conferences and interviews. There *are* times when a chunk of verbatim in a story is more effective than a summary, however beautifully written.

I'm sorry, I'll write that again

The most damning thing a sub can say about his own work is "Well, I didn't understand it either, but that's what the man said." Make this an absolute rule: **IF YOU DON'T UNDERSTAND IT, DON'T PUT IT IN AS IT STANDS.**

The sub must either knock it out if it doesn't matter, or start inquiries if it seems to have any significance. I wonder if the reporter who wrote the sentence that follows, or the sub who let it through, really knew what it meant:

The point to be borne in mind was that they had to consider the general viability of the locality within which the decline was taking place.

A junior Minister talking, of course. He was answering, or rather *not* answering, a straight question about aid for a "grey" area. One thing's for sure: the man most affected, standing in the dole queue, wouldn't understand it.

It is in official statements that meaninglessness is developed to a fine art:

The new baths will be built subject to the provisions of the Act . . .

A sub must explain what the Act provides.

The council decided to precept on the rating authority for these sums . . .

A sub must explain whether the rates are up or down.

An epitome of accounts submitted by the Borough Treasurer . . .

A sub must explain what an epitome of accounts is.

These are simple things, and the sub will be able to turn them into English without seeking aid. But suppose he is faced with a lump of stodge like this:

He said that the object was to progressively orientate the subject towards a feeling of integration and eliminate the dichotomy created in its personality by the presence of a black–white clash relationship.

This sort of verbal cotton wool is intolerable in a popular newspaper, and unless it can be explained in simple English it just has to go.

That's OK by me, brother

One thing that every sub has to learn quickly is that in achieving simplicity he must follow the style and mood of the newspaper. If the newspaper insists on a formality that seems to him stiff and pedantic, so be it. There is little he can do about it short of buying a controlling interest in the company. If, on the other hand, a degree of flexibility is allowed, he needs to know how far he can go without causing a great reaction to set in.

Take the question of contractions. It will be noted that in the story about Mrs Belcher above I have used the contractions *she'd* and *wouldn't.* No doubt there are editors and proprietors who deplore this, and long may their products prosper. But many newspapers allow contractions *in a certain kind of story.*

The view is taken that it's fine to begin a chatty, jolly story

Mrs Minnie Nuttle got her finger stuck in the mangle yesterday — and couldn't get it out

because to say *could not* somehow spoils the atmosphere.

But equally, it can be argued, there is something out of character about using *wouldn't* in a sentence like this in a formal (non-sketch) Parliamentary report:

The Prime Minister wouldn't reveal what he said during his talks with the U.S. President.

The sub must establish by reading his own newspaper (and to a certain extent by trial and error) what kinds of limits he is working within. This also applies in other fields.

SLANG may be banned completely or allowed in some contexts. Subject to the general policy laid down, the sub's guideline must be: Does it add to the readability of the story? In some cases it may well do so because it is in keeping with the mood:

Old Bill Sludge, a night watchman for 50 years, got a right going-over when he arrived for work an hour late yesterday. The boss didn't know he'd become a hero on the way — and Bill was too shy to tell him.

But some papers would rule out "a right going-over". Some would even rule out "the boss". It is important for the sub to know where his own paper draws the line.

AMERICANISMS present a similar problem. I am personally convinced that the American influence is now so strong that it is useless to fight on and on. A newspaper needs to speak in the language of its readers. If it fails to, the readers won't change: they'll just change their newspaper.

It follows from this that some newspapers can stand Canute-like against this "corruption" of the English language, although the grave is against them. What newspaper bans *teenage* now? But the popular paper has to bear in mind the constantly-changing idiom, particularly in relation to the barrage of American films and TV programmes. A reference to someone "wanting out" was deleted from a story yesterday — but will it be deleted tomorrow?

There are really two aspects to the admission of Americanisms — how far they have been accepted into the language of the immediate audience, and how far the newspaper is prepared to recognise the acceptance. It is the second that is the more important from the sub's point of view.

CLICHES are treated with varying degrees of hostility, and I think it is important for the sub to distinguish between the really tired old things like blushing bride and tender mercies, and valuable new portmanteau phrases which are occasionally introduced into the language.

No sub should allow through intros like these:

Faces were red at St George's Young Wives meeting last Wednesday when . . .

An accident to the bridegroom on the way to a wedding proved a blessing in disguise at Saddleworth on Saturday . . .

Mr Ezra Snout, for many years a tower of strength to Tintwistle Band of Hope, celebrated his . . .

But cliché-chopping ought not to get out of hand. In many cases the cliché is the warm, familiar phrase that the reader recognises, that *puts things in a nutshell.*

This particularly applies to some of the dramatic phrases coined in recent years. Winston Churchill's *iron curtain* has been both over-used and outdated by events, but for years it expressed in two simple words a complicated situation. Over-exposure has turned Macmillan's *wind of change* into a cliché, but it remains meaningful. What tortuous phrases do we need to avoid using *cold war?*

I have given elsewhere the classic example of Mr Edwin Gay, until his death the diligent revise sub of the *Daily Mail*, who during a wild bout of cliché-hunting suddenly conceived a frenzied dislike of *kiss of life*. Now in my view no more admirable cliché has arrived on the scene during my time in newspapers. It expresses precisely what is meant; it brings a picture of the scene into the reader's mind. The fact that it is the obvious phrase is no disadvantage. Why search for some inferior alternative when it is not necessary?

The rule should be: if it's the tired, automatic phrase that just crept in — have it out; but if it expresses exactly an idea, let it stand.

Where has all the clumsiness gone?

I thought it might be worth while to take one example which demonstrates some of the faults referred to above, point them out, and then reduce the story to a simple straightforward form. It is not a piece of raw copy, but a story published in a local newspaper on the day this was written. Only the name of the paper has been changed.

FOR tape recording enthusiast Mr Frank Morten, it was the first time he had entered such a contest after a competition offering a prize of a £500 video-recorder caught his eye in an Independent Television magazine.

Note involved, clumsy construction and inversion in opening sentence. "Such a contest" as what? Cliché: Caught his eye.

That was some two months ago, but recently, Mr Morten, of "Elderwood," 62 Corbar Road, was overjoyed to hear the news that he had gained first place and so won the "Sony video-recorder," which enables him to record sound and vision off television.

Why "some"? When is recently? Why house name *and* number? Cliché: Was overjoyed to hear. 44-word sentence.

And at the week-end he and his wife travelled overnight to the Midland Television studios at Birmingham, where he received the award from, coincidentally, a television announcer named Miss Jean Morton.

Why "And"? Note *television* twice and archaic *coincidentally:* different spelling of name anyway.

Speaking of his astonishment at winning such a prize, at the first attempt, Mr Morten told the *Town Crier:*

First 13 words repetitious and unnecessary.

"I had seen these in the shops, but never thought I would ever have one."

"These" ungrammatical. Video-recorders (pl) not previously mentioned.

In the competition, he explained, there were set out 20 news items of local interest. Competitors had to imagine these were to be shown to patients in hospital, and pick out what they considered the most suitable ten.

Unnecessarily verbose.

He went on: "First we received a letter telling us we had tied with several others, and would I select a further two items from the remaining ten for elimination purposes."

Ungrammatical (should be "asking if I would") and verbose. Note jargon "elimination purposes".

This he did, and after a telephone call he was visited by a representative of the magazine and informed of his success.

Verbose. Note "formal word" *informed.*

Mr Morten said he and his wife travelled to the Birmingham studios overnight last Friday, as they had to be there for nine o'clock on Saturday morning.

Virtual repeat of paragraph 3.

"They gave us a wonderful time there," remarked Mr Morten, "showed us round the studios, and brought us home by car with the equipment."

Starts with statement of obvious. Note odd choice of *remarked.*

Both Mr and Mrs Morten have a keen interest in tape recording, and are members of the National Tape Club, World Wide Tape Talk (two British organisations), and World Tapes for Education, an American club.

Note "automatic adjective" keen. Phrase unnecessary anyway, because unless they were interested they wouldn't join the societies.

A commercial advertising the magazine will feature the couple receiving the prize on Midlands television some time later this week—Wednesday or Thursday, it is thought.

Why "some time"? Who thinks "it is thought"? — an intolerable phrase for a newspaper.

Now let us look how the story might have been told, without repetition with the utmost simplicity, and in a form the reader would absorb at first go. The original version is repeated for comparison. The exact sequence has been kept deliberately.

FOR tape recording enthusiast Mr Frank Morten, it was the first time he had entered such a contest after a competition offering a prize of a £500 video-recorder caught his eye in an Independent Television magazine.

That was some two months ago, but recently, Mr Morten, of "Elderwood," 62 Corbar Road, was overjoyed to hear the news that he had gained first place and so won the "Sony video recorder," which enables him to record sound and vision off television.

And at the week-end he and his wife travelled overnight to the Midland Television studios at Birmingham, where he received the award from, coincidentally, a television announcer named Miss Jean Morton.

Speaking of his astonishment at winning such a prize, at the first attempt, Mr Morten told the *Town Crier:*

"I had seen these in the shops, but never thought I would ever have one."

In the competition, he explained, there were set out 20 news items of local interest. Competitors had to

TAPE recording enthusiast Mr Frank Morten has won a £500 video-recorder in a contest run by an ITV magazine.

Mr Morten, of 62 Corbar Road, received the award in Birmingham on Saturday from TV personality Jean Morton. He said: "I've seen video-recorders in the shops but I never thought I'd have one".

Competitors were asked to decide which ten of 20 local news items were of most interest to hospital patients. Mr Morten tied with other contestants and later successfully eliminated another two items.

He and his wife were shown round the studios and then driven home with the equipment.

Mr and Mrs Morten are members of the British National Tape Club and World Wide Tape Talk, and the American club World Tapes for Education. They will be seen receiving the awards on Midlands TV this week.

imagine these were to be shown to patients in hospital, and pick out what they considered the most suitable ten.

He went on : "First we received a letter telling us we had tied with several others, and would I select a further two items from the remaining ten for elimination purposes."

This he did, and after a telephone call he was visited by a representative of the magazine and informed of his success.

Mr Morten said he and his wife travelled to the Birmingham studios overnight last Friday, as they had to be there for nine o'clock on Saturday morning.

"They gave us a wonderful time there," remarked Mr Morten, "showed us round the studios, and brought us home by car with the equipment."

Both Mr and Mrs Morten have a keen interest in tape recording, and are members of the National Tape Club, World Wide Tape Talk (two British organizations), and World Tapes for Education, an American club.

A commercial advertising the magazine will feature the couple receiving the prize on Midlands television some time later this week— Wednesday or Thursday, it is thought.

In the new version the story is much simpler and easier to read, the repetition has been removed, and the length has been reduced without losing one thought that matters. There is room underneath for another story, or space to expand the existing one with details that contribute something.

Tomorrow is another day

A well-subbed story is an ephemeral thing. There are no awards for the best subbing operation of the year. The odds are that if a sub does a great job on a story the reporter will get the credit for it anyway.

For this reason many subs adopt the quite-understandable attitude that once the copy has left their hands that's it. That may well be, but it ought not to be.

Some subs have a greater capacity than others for returning to the scene and improving on a masterpiece. I recall being lost in admiration at the way a colleague on the *Daily Mail,* used to return first to galley proofs then to page proofs, seeking words that could be removed or improved, sentences that could be simplified or polished, intros that could be sharpened, facts that could be checked.

Not many men have this capacity, and indeed it's possible to be a good and useful sub without possessing it to this extent. But it ought to be cultivated.

If it's something you
know about – it's wrong

It has been rightly said, and by me, that the road back to down-table subbing on obscure newspapers for the union minimum is paved with dropped bricks. The quality more important than any other in a sub's work is **ACCURACY**. Genius he can do without, slowness can be overcome, bad spelling will be caught somewhere along the line — but a capacity to check and check and check is vital.

There is some truth in the old saying that if you have personal knowledge of any story in a newspaper you'll find a mistake in it. Some of the errors arise out of a lack of understanding of the subject, some out of difficulties and obstructions put in the way of the reporter, but most out of the fact that no two people see things in the same way.

This last kind of inaccuracy has its source in the information given to the newspaper, and the newspaper is wrongly blamed for it. Television, with its live interviews, is fortunate in not suffering in the same way. If BBC and ITV interview two different witnesses of a bank robbery and they tell conflicting stories (as they often do) any doubt about their authenticity rubs off on them. But if the *Daily Express* story is based on the evidence of one and the *Daily Mail* story on the evidence of the other and clashing headlines appear—

JENNIE	DUSTMAN
THE CHAR	CHARLIE
FOILS	FOILS
RAIDERS	RAIDERS

then it is assumed that one or other newspaper has invented the story. In fact they have both relied on eye-witnesses and the apparent discrepancy is probably merely a matter of emphasis.

I remember once handling a story about a film star being blown up at a fireworks party. Three people present gave three versions:

She was blown out of the window.

She was thrown out of the window by some big strong man who was present.

She fled screaming from the room.

We chose what seemed to be the most reliable witness, and went on his word. Other papers chose others. The result was that three different versions appeared in the newspapers, and the cynics produced this as an example of the unreliability of the Press. In fact, if anyone did any inventing it was probably the publicity-conscious mob at the party, who would undoubtedly have blown up anyone to get in the papers.

This kind of inaccuracy is a cross that newspapers have to bear. It is beyond their power to do anything about it. But one thing can be laid down absolutely: nothing that is checkable ought to go unchecked. If a name, place, age or title goes in incorrectly then the newspaper, and more particularly the sub-editor, is at fault.

It is not that newspapermen are particularly prone to this kind of error, but just that they have more opportunity than most. The Health Service folk sent me a new medical card covering a change of doctor. In spite of my letter to them being typed they have managed to get two mistakes in three words (Sellars for Sellers, Cedars House for Cedar House). Until this moment no one but me knew about it. But if a newspaper makes mistakes like that large numbers of people will know and the paper will be subject to the customary hatred, ridicule and contempt.

A newspaper is exceptionally vulnerable in these things. Spell a man's name incorrectly and he will be deeply hurt, because it's all his own, and he will spread the news around. Leave the hyphen out of the name of a town, or put it in the wrong county, and the sneers will be audible to all. Make a mistake in a title and the U-people will be convinced that they were right about your station in life. Only the sub can save his newspaper from the ill-repute that follows such mistakes. And the sub's only safeguard lies in the celebrated Beaverbrook phrase:

DON'T TRUST TO LUCK.

Don't even trust staff copy typed in the office. I *know* that it should be possible to trust it, and the fact that it sometimes isn't possible can be a source of bitterness to subs. I've long held the view that if a mistake appears in reporter-typed copy then the biggest kick ought to go to the reporter, but it doesn't happen. The sub must therefore watch for warning signals — the wrongly-spelt name, the misused title — that alerts him to the need to check everything else.

The sections that follow are each headed with quotes that contain warning-light mistakes.

Not Wislon, you fool

**Sir Basil Smallpiece found a diamond in
the ninth of a dozen oysters he was
eating at the Savoy Grill yesterday.**

The name should be SMALLPEICE. It is one of the names that
regularly appear incorrectly in newspapers. (I've even known it happen in
the City section of the *Sunday Telegraph.*)

There are some names which are particularly accident-prone. One of
Britain's great political writers always used to type a capital L in the middle
of the great Iain Macleod's name, and another of the same ilk spelt his
Christian name *Ian*. I always have to check whether the Queen's daughter
is Ann or Anne.

Is the sub absolutely sure whether it's:

> *Julian Amory or Julian Amery?*
> *Lord Boyd-Orr or Lord Boyd Orr?*
> *Chevenix-Trench or Chenevic-Trench?*
> *Rupert de la Bere or Rupert De la Bere?*
> *Walter De La Mare or Walter de la Mare?*
> *Earl De la Warr or Earl De La Warr?*
> *Frankie Howard or Frankie Howerd?*
> *Trevor Howerd or Trevor Howard?*
> *Earl of Middleton or Earl of Midleton?*
> *Lord Midleton or Lord Middleton?*

Watch particularly these two groups of people:

ALL THE MACS AND McS. They are easy to get wrong and the victims
get so angry if they get the wrong prefix or a lower case letter where it
should be a cap.

ALL HYPHENATED NAMES, particularly in those cases where some
members of a family use a hyphen and others don't. (Only Charles among
the Chenevix-Trenches, for example, drops the hyphen.) No sub could
possibly know all these things off pat. Therefore he must check that the
reporter has got it right. Here the reference books come into their own.
For names of well-known people the best sources are:

Who's Who

Kelly's Handbook to the Titled, Landed and Official Classes, which
contains a lot of names not in *Who's Who,* such as JPs, retired officers, and
holders of courtesy titles.

Who's Who in America.

International Who's Who.

If the people concerned are known in specialist fields but are unlikely to be in general reference books there are many other sources:

Medical Directory for doctors
Law List for barristers and solicitors
Directory of British Scientists
Navy List
Army List
Air Force List
Who's Who in the Theatre
Who's Who in Music
Author's and Writer's Who's Who
TV and Radio Who's Who
Crockford's Clerical Directory for the Church of England and similar books for other churches.
Civil Service List
Foreign Office List
Colonial Office List

If the character concerned is dead then there are the accumulated volumes of:

Who Was Who?

With the really unknown, there are still many sources available:

Kelly's Directories, which list householders in alphabetical order, and list streets in alphabetical order with residents' names.

The Electoral Roll

and, of course, in these affluent days, the phone books kindly provided free by British Telecom.

Good lord — not him

Lord Cohen spoke to the General Medical Council yesterday of problems facing doctors.

It wasn't Lord Cohen, but an entirely different chap called Lord Cohen of Birkenhead. Lord Cohen, a life peer, is a distinguished lawyer and as far as I know has no connection at all with the medical profession.

The importance of distinguishing between peers of the same name is becoming increasingly important because there are now more of them as new life peers are constantly created. There was a case in which a newspaper attributed a daughter to Lord Lloyd, who is an Old Etonian banker, former Lord-in-Waiting to the Queen, and the second baron. The lass had in fact been sired by Lord Lloyd of Hampstead, a legal gentleman created a life peer during the reign of H Wilson. Not surprisingly Lord Lloyd protested.

All peers are *of* somewhere, but in most cases the *of* is not part of the title. Exceptions are where newly-ennobled chaps are allowed by the Crown to have their title forever associated with some particular spot (Montgomery of Alamein), and where there would be a confusion between two peers of the same or similar names.

The quick, sharp key for all subs is

Who's Who

because it gives the "of somewhere" in bold type to distinguish it if it should be used.

Outrage at Salford, Yorks

A mother and four children were killed yesterday when a chip shop blew up in Moreton-in-the-Marsh, Worcestershire.

The place is actually Moreton-in-Marsh, and it's in Gloucestershire anyway. Nothing so upsets a customer as having his home town wrongly rendered, unless it's having his name bodged up.

No town or village about which there is the slightest doubt should go unchecked. I don't suggest that the sub should call for the gazetteer every time he sees L-O-N-D-O-N in copy. He's not, after all, a member of a union working to rule. But he must watch particularly for three things:

1. Has he got the place in the right county? Peak Dale (Derbyshire) has the postal address "Stockport, Cheshire", but if the sub puts it in Cheshire he makes enemies. And is Todmorden in Lancashire or Yorkshire? That's a real problem.

2. Has he got an apostrophe, or omitted an apostrophe, if that's the case? Is it

Bishops Stortford?   *Hogs Back?*

Connahs Quay?   *John O'Groats?*

Or alternatively is it

Husband's Bosworth?   *Pett's Wood?*

It's not any of them. They're all WRONG.

3. Does a compound name have hyphens or not, and is the conjunction correct? Is it Newcastle on Tyne, or Newcastle-on-Tyne, or Newcastle-upon-Tyne or Newcastle upon Tyne? (The last is correct.) Can the sub be sure, without checking, that he's got these right:

Ashton in Makerfield?   *Stockton-on-Tees?*

Clayton-le-Moors?   *Stoke by Nayland?*

Newcastle-under-Lyme?   *Stow-on-the-Wold?*

If he's got them as they appear above, they're all CORRECT.

Best check-books on geographical points:

Bartholomew's Survey Gazetteer of the British Isles, which lists even the tiniest hamlets and pinpoints the nearest place anyone has ever heard of.

Post Office Guide, issued once a year.

The Times Atlas and World Gazetteer.

Warning: Do not rely for these matters on the *AA Member's Handbook.* It tends to be a bit erratic on the finer points.

Sorry, your reverence

The Vicar of Pintwistle, the Reverend Groger-Evans, fell head first into the font at a christening at St Mark's Church yesterday.

The title "the Reverend" must be followed by a Christian name or initials, and the story should therefore read "The Reverend George Groger-Evans . . ." or "The Reverend G R Groger-Evans . . .". It is correct but both undesirable and archaic to say "The Reverend Mr Groger-Evans . . .".

Most subs usually avoid the most notorious mistakes, such as calling Nonconformist ministers *priests* (they never regard their function as priestly) or referring to them as *vicars* or *rectors.* (Both titles refer to specific offices which the Nonconformist churches don't have.)

But other mistakes, such as calling a bishop "Very Reverend" (he's "Right Reverend"), or calling all Jewish clergymen "Rabbi" (most of them are "the Reverend"), do creep in at times.

For checks on the names and status of individuals in the various churches, these are the main reference books:

Crockford's Clerical Directory, published alternate years, which lists all Anglican clergymen with biographical details, and their parishes

The Catholic Directory, which does a similar job for the Roman Catholic Church

The Free Church Directory
The Year Book of the Methodist Conference
The Baptist Handbook
The Congregational Year Book
The Jewish Year Book.

Lord Bernard Norfolk and all that

Lord Ted Willis announced from his Chislehurst home yesterday that Sergeant Dixon of Dock Green was to marry Mrs Thursday.

He can't be Lord Ted Willis, because that would make him the son of a duke, marquis, or earl. They are the only people who have titles "Lord, Christian name, Surname" and these are held as a courtesy.

So the sub has to get round it by saying Lord Willis (playwright Ted Willis) or cheat and say Lord "Ted" Willis so that the reader knows who is being talked about.

The best check-book is:

Kelly's Handbook of Titled, Landed and Official Classes which lists all titled folk in alphabetical order. Miss Jan Reid, the noted journalistic authority on such matters, points out that this volume is exceptionally useful because it has more ex-directory telephone numbers than any other.*

Also valuable:

Debrett's Peerage, which is sectionalised according to ranks — peers and families, courtesy titles, Privy Councillors, baronets, knights and knights' widows. But it's very handy for spotting heirs, because their names are in caps.

Burke's Peerage gives a fuller family history and lists the dead as well as the living. Peers and baronets have one section, knights another, and there is also a section on extinct titles.

Dod's Parliamentary Companion and *Vacher's Parliamentary Companion* both list peers alphabetically. The first gives biographies, too. The second also lists peers according to rank and seniority.

All that glisters . . .

Mr Caliaghan added sagely:
"Money is the root of all evil."

He may well have done in the state that the poor chap got himself into, but what the Bible actually said is *"The love* of money is the root of all evil", and customers won't be slow to point it out.

Misquotations always bring in complaints from the erudite. The firm rule should be. **NEVER USE A QUOTATION WITHOUT CHECKING IT — EVEN IF YOU THINK YOU'RE SURE.**

Best reference books:

Oxford Book of Quotations
Everyman's Dictionary of Quotations and Proverbs
Benham's Book of Quotations
Stevenson's Book of Quotations
Oxford Dictionary of Proverbs
Penguin Dictionary of Quotations

---

*But not, I rush to say, more than Miss Jan Reid.

For Bible references (and this can save an awful lot of work), there is
Cruden's Concordance
and for The Bard himself
Shakespeare Concordance

Not just the mayor

**Among the distinguished guests present
was the Mayor of Bradford . . .**

Actually it was the Lord Mayor (they've had one since 1907) and
Yorkshiremen everywhere are enraged by the indignity he has suffered.
These things always need checking if they appear at all marginal — I, for
example, expect Cambridge and Canterbury to have a Lord Mayor apiece,
but they don't.

The best check-book for any facts about local authorities is
The Municipal Year Book
which is crammed with the names of officials, the rates they extort, areas
and population, and suchlike gems.

The Education Committees Year Book fills in some of the gaps left.

Is that a record?

**Lord Salisbury, who was elevated to
Lord President of the Council by Eden . . .**

He wasn't, because he held the office under Churchill, as the sub would
have seen if he'd checked in
Whitaker's Almanack
which really is the main book to turn to for all sorts of information. It's
published every year and covers an amazing variety of topics:

> Tide tables and trade unions
> Cabinet Ministers past and present
> Divorce statistics and crime figures
> Passport regulations and houses open to the public
> Service pay and rail routes
> Tablespoon measures and Nobel prize winners
> Law Courts and Sterling balances
> Records and resignations
> Charitable bequests and top archers

hundreds of tightly-packed pages, not only on everything under the sun,
but on the sun itself, which has dozens of entries of its own.

Private, not public

Boys at Christ's College, the public school in fashionable Blackheath, were yesterday . . .

It may have been founded in 1823 and have a lovely crest but it's not a public school in the normal usage of the phrase. For boys' schools the term is restricted to those which are members of the Headmasters' Conference, from Eton upwards or downwards. The rest are independent schools.

Full details on all the public schools are in the
Public and Preparatory Schools Year Book.

One caution on reference books: Make sure the one you're using is up to date. The words of W Shakespeare are changeless, but the last available *Who's Who* in an office I visited recently described the late Lord George-Brown, as Joint Parliamentary Secretary, Min of Ag and Fish.

That's a capital suggestion

Even assuming that everything checkable has been checked, there are still perils that lie in wait. The greatest of these is bad writing. "Night Lawyer", who contributes excellent articles to *U.K Press Gazette,* made the point this way:

"I have found that many errors are caused by physical means which cannot properly be described as negligence. Bad handwriting by sub-editors is one cause.

"I suppose it is a kind of negligence to send copy down to the caseroom which is not clear, and this bad handwriting business is only part of the dirty copy trouble which is, in my view, one of the most frequent causes of errors in newspapers, and one which can quite definitely be improved if not completely overcome. The trouble with it is that everyone concerned accepts it.

"Of course, we have correctors of the Press and the number of times they have saved the situation is incalculable. But metal drops, and goes into the page and it is moulded very often before the readers have been through the galley . . .

"Someone climbing between the rollers of a rotary to chip or bash a plate because of a ghastly mistake just spotted by the reader is something most subs of any experience have watched many times. And the chances are that dirty copy caused it."

He's right and every sub knows that he's right, however filthy his own handwriting might be.

Many of the worst mistakes can be avoided by CAPPING ALL PROPER NAMES, of towns and products as well as people. It is a good idea, also, to follow any unusual form with the ringed word "correct":

Miss Mai (*correct*) *Slopstone*

Mr Horatio Stewarte (*correct*)

Dirty proofs I have dealt with above. No sub should forget that if any name or figure appears incorrectly in a galley proof, and he makes a mark involving a reset, the mistake is quite likely to be perpetuated.

It's a good thing to cultivate an eye for errors in proofs, particularly page proofs. Some questions to ask as the eye moves over the page:

Are all the headings in good shape? Not too squashed against the rules? Most important: HAVE YOU CUT THE HEADLINE POINT OUT OF THE STORY?

Are all the crossheads and sideheads covered? Are they correctly positioned from a visual *and* a sense point of view?

Are the pictures in the right places, or have they got pushed too near other pictures? Most important: HAVE YOU SEEN AN IDENT AND MADE SURE THE RIGHT CAPTION IS ON THE RIGHT PICTURE?

Are there any missing lines, particularly at the beginning and end of paragraphs?

Is there any wrong measure?

Are all the rules and cut-offs where they should be? Have tie-on stories been accidentally cut off, or have stories that should have been cut off been tied in?

Are there any ugly turns of half a line into the next leg of a story that doubles up, and if so has the reset already gone out?

Are all the datelines on the stories they were intended for?

If a story turns to another page is the turn-over slug correct?

Are there any wrong founts or literals that the Printer or readers should have spotted? In *The Times* itself I saw its sister referred to as

The Sinday Times

thus providing two embrarrassing faults in one line.

Are there any clashes, either typographically or verbally, with adjacent headings? Imagine the anguish at the late London *Evening News* when they followed the tragic story

ESCALATOR GIRL LOSES LEG

with one of those punny ha-ha stories they love so much:

Caught on the hop

He admitted that he hadn't got a leg
to stand on—Woolwich witness.

Absolutely vital, because if you let this one go the row will reverberate for weeks: Have you got a story about an industrialist's appalling behaviour sitting on an ad placed by his company?

Always keep an eye on the ads. No newspaper is going to suppress an official report on smoking and lung cancer, but the one that wraps it round a cigarette ad is guilty of what Mao's lads called a filthy provocation.

Beware the gobbledygook, my son, and shun . . .

READ the quote that follows with care. Let it be a text for all sub-editors, not to guide them in the paths of righteousness but to warn them of what lies in wait for all those who fall victim to jargon.

The Indian Government is giving active consideration to the containerisation and palletisation of bones exported to Britain for the making of gelatine in a bid to minimise the danger of anthrax.

Savour these bureaucratic jewels:

> *Containerisation*
> *Palletisation*
> *Minimise*

And these circumlocutions:

> *Giving active consideration to*
> *For the making of*

And finally one of the great overworked phrases of our time:

> *In a bid to*

The dreadful thing is that it's so easy to say the same thing in English:

India is considering improved packing for bones sent to British gelatine firms to cut the danger of anthrax.

Not a beautiful sentence. But at any rate one that is shorter, clearer, and free of all contamination by the jargoneers.

The story that followed this intro was full of similar tired phrases beloved of those who have grown old writing letters from Ministries and town halls. What was the Indian Government doing? Giving the matter priority consideration. What then? Measures would be put in hand. What was their attitude? They were obviously alive to the problem.

The story only came to life at the end, when one of the chaps concerned was asked what he thought of the suggestion that the Indians were slipping in a few human bones to make up the weight. "*I think that's a load of piffle*" he said.

That sentence provides the rule which should guide all sub-editors: faced with jargon in whatever form it appears. He must say to himself: **I THINK THAT'S A LOAD OF PIFFLE.** And he must then go on to cut it out or turn it into language the average chap can understand.

Reference Form CO2/H2S04/K9P

The example quoted suffers mainly from the language of the bureaucrats — officialese, the dreaded gobbledygook. All sub-editors by now must be aware of the perils of talking about accommodation units when they mean houses and flats. But what of these:

Methods of inter-city transportation were discussed yesterday when . . .
They mean transport.
Five thousand railwaymen will become redundant as a result of . . .
They mean they'll be sacked.
The proliferation of nuclear weapons among small nations . . .
They mean the spread.
The implementation of an agreement to solve the "who-batters-what" dispute in fish-and-chip shops was delayed last night . . .
They mean the operation.
The blueprint for a new town centre for Broadbottom . . .
They mean the plan.
The figure of short-term unemployed . . .
They mean temporarily out of work.
A ceiling of 50p was set on the price of fish fingers to deal with the problems of short supply . . .
They mean a top price of 50p was fixed because fish fingers are scarce.
New criteria to assess the value of productivity agreements . . .
They mean new ways.
The end product will be a loss of potency . . .
They mean the result but they're right about the loss of potency. The written word certainly loses potency when this kind of jargon is introduced.
Observe its effect in this intro:
A reference has been made today to the National Board for Prices and Incomes of the margins of distributors, in the event of an increase attributable to devaluation in the manufacturer's price, on those goods for which prices for resale are customarily recommended.
The astonishing thing is that when its meaning was discovered it became a big Page One story.
Possibly an even greater danger, because it's easier to let through, is waffle-jargon — the introduction of words that mean absolutely nothing.

This was the intro on a story about the Far East crisis:

The riddle of Asia got more and more baffling today. Things were happening so swiftly and so bewilderingly that they raised conjecture to the highest point yet.

At any rate the bafflement was conveyed to the reader.

This was extracted from a story about the Cyprus crisis:

Experts in London are clearly hoping that nothing will be said to worsen the crisis.

Note the anonymity of the experts, sitting there with clear minds, without even thoughts in them. Foreign Office spokesmen may well be hired to think up meaningless platitudes. Subs are hired to make sure they don't get in the newspaper.

At the other end of the scale is the political-abuse jargon, in which the meaning of words is stretched to breaking-point. Quote from *Izvestia*, also on the Cyprus crisis:

The black deeds of the greedy reactionaries reek of Hitlerism and the evil Inquisition.

This kind of thing, when it appears in its extreme form, is all right for the occasional giggle, in quote marks. But subs must beware of introducing these jargon words as though they were the newspaper's own.

Old Slippery Elm, as Mr Bernard Levin described a well-known politician in his shockingly disrespectful way, converted certain words like pragmatic and purposive into meaningless gobbledygook. One reactionary MP even attempted a dictionary of these sayings:

"Meaningful" — What I want something to mean.

"Meaningless" — Something unpleasant I'd rather you ignored.

"Dynamic new initiative" — Another new gimmick on the way.

"I'm going to be perfectly frank and honest" — Run for cover.

"Rhodesian sanctions are a great moral issue" — As long as they don't affect our trade with South Africa.

"I want to be quite clear on this; there will be no devaluation" — Sell Sterling.

As Humpty Dumpty said to Alice: "When I use a word it means just what I choose it to mean — neither more nor less." Words that mean anything anyone chooses them to mean have no place in a newspaper.

See you at luncheon, Daphne

Another group of words to avoid are those that reek of pomposity: the formal, polysyllabic, posh words used by the mayor opening the annual Women's Institute Christmas Fayre. Wherever possible the sub should convert them to the words used in everyday speech.

The bride was attired in . . .
No: the bride wore.
The sale raised approximately £15 . . .
No: about £15.
Police constable Chamberlayne then observed . . .
No: he saw.
The reception was at the bride's residence . . .
No: her home.
Prior to the luncheon . . .
No: before lunch.
The objective was to assist the necessitous . . .
No: the aim was to help the needy.
He endeavoured to suborn the chief sub . . .
No: he tried to bribe the swine.
They had attempted to expedite what they regarded as a viable plan . . .
No: they had tried to speed up what they thought a workable plan.

There are dozens more that creep in: veritable for real, inform for tell, objective for aim, require for want, terminate for end, purchase for buy, conceal for hide, acquire for get, ameliorate for improve, evince for show, peruse for read, ascertain for find out, cease for stop, donation for gift, commence for begin.

Words like these can be found in speeches and reports from all organisations which incline to the pompous. This Leaden Treasury comes from just such a set-up:

". . . one of the association's *stalwarts*, who *rendered sterling service* when he was *resident* in London, *passed away* on the 8th November. A *floral tribute* and a letter of *condolence* have been sent *on the association's behalf*."

If any of the words in italic survive, the sub is not doing his job.

Burly union bosses and others

Regrettably, not only civil servants and mayors create jargon. Newspapermen do it too. The problem arises out of the overuse of convenience words — those simple, pithy phrases which quickly sum up a man or a thing or a situation. Because they're so handy they tend to recur monotonously, and are even at times dropped in where they're not applicable.

I have reached the stage of wincing whenever I see union leaders described as *burly*. Faced with a *neat* semi-detached house I struck out *neat*: I had no means of knowing whether it was really neat or whether the reporter just couldn't stop himself typing it. Consider this example of the new journalese:

Hero of the raid, 37-year-old Theodore Clutch, dialled 999 to report that the bandits — both teenagers — were still in the shop. Police who dashed through rush-hour traffic faced a headache when they arrived on the scene.

Four examples of words that ought to be used only with extreme care.

HERO, so easy to debase, here used of a man who did no more than phone the police.

BANDIT, a word not devoid of glamour, here used of a couple of young hooligans.

DASHED, an impossibility in rush-hour traffic, a convenience word both overused and misused.

HEADACHE, an example of habit jargon, used to dramatise the slightest problem and so losing all its force.

Another example:

Top Welsh Conservative Mr Allen Howl shocked party members last night with the bombshell announcement that he was to quit the chairmanship of Llareggub Primrose League after being rapped for his attitude to the Common Market.

TOP, a word thrown in with abandon to make the story seem more impressive than it is.

SHOCKED, not kept for occasions when something shocking happens, but trotted out to cover anything even mildly surprising.

BOMBSHELL, the new-journalese substitute for sensational, another mark of an overplayed story.

QUIT, a convenience word for headlines, which now threatens in some newspapers to eliminate altogether perfectly good words such as *resign* and *leave*.

RAPPED, trotted out to dramatise the mildest rebuke or even disagreement.

From all these, and from luxury flats, revolutionary breakthroughs, grim-faced delegates, overwhelming defeats, high-ranking civil servants, million-strong organisations, rushing fire-brigades, mercy-dashing ambulances, bids, bans, probes, blasts, spaghetti kings, meccas, marathons, pacts, ordeals and problems, the sub should protect the reader. Not exclude them completely: that is the counsel of absurdity. But use them with such care that there is no danger of the currency being debased.

The sub should also, unless he is doing a Saturday stint on *The Observer*, avoid cult words that will baffle the reader and give him a feeling of inferiority. He may himself be a diligent reader of the *New Statesman*, in which case gems like ambience and dichotomy will be constantly on his lips. But his job as a sub is to make it unnecessary for the railway porter or the borer and grinder to reach for a dictionary. When he is faced in a news story with

causal	*empathy*	*seminal*
charisma	*milieu*	*symbiosis*
coeval	*mores*	*thematic*

and all their kindred spirits, his only course is to translate or strike them out.

Beware, too, of the jargon of the technological age. The British end of Honeywell, the U.S. computer giant, produced this magnificent "Instant Buzzword Generator". You simply take one word from each column and run them together, and "command instant respect" for your in-ness.

Column 1	Column 2	Column 3
0. integrated	0. management	0. options
1. total	1. organisational	1. flexibility
2. systematised	2. monitored	2. capability
3. parallel	3. reciprocal	3. mobility
4. functional	4. digital	4. programming
5. responsive	5. logic	5. concept
6. optical	6. transitional	6. time-phase
7. synchronised	7. incremental	7. projection
8. compatible	8. third-generation	8. hardware
9. balanced	9. policy	9. contingency

If you find yourself writing "parallel policy options" or "systematised organisational mobility" — watch it.

One final note, which in the strictest sense is outside the gobbledygook theme: Subs should avoid the ghastly euphemisms which almost daily overtake each other. America is becoming a fantastic source of this genteelism, which is rather surprising. Miss Anne Scott-James summed it up beautifully after a visit there:

They never call a spade a spade if they can find some daintier way of putting it. I choose from my large collection:

"Motion discomfort" for airsickness.

"Selective patronage" for a tough trade boycott.

And a wondrous variety of words for hotel lavatories. My favourites are Squires and Damsels, Masters and Mistresses, Dukes and Duchesses. Feeling unqualified to enter this last, I held out till we got home.

When the Queen bites that dog — it's news

The Duchess of Dinting, five-times-married cousin of the Queen, was arrested in a strip club early today and accused of a £1,000,000 plot to defraud the Archbishop of Canterbury.

Now there's an intro for you. It's got high-life (not merely a duchess but a cousin of H M), sex (five-times-married *and* a strip club), living-it-upness (early today), money (a million pounds of it), crime (a plot), and religion (the Archbishop).

Of course, it falls to few of us to ball-point 31 such lovely words. But this intro has virtues which provide a guide for less-exciting tales.

IT IS SIMPLE, clear and direct.

EVERY WORD in it does some work.

IT ANSWERS those questions tiresome readers ask — Who? What? When? Where? Why?

It also has one other, overriding virtue — that which was so firmly laid down by Northcliffe. One dictum of his survives unchanging and unchallenged.

NEWS IS ANYTHING OUT OF THE ORDINARY.

This, above all, is the thing that matters. Clarity, yes. Tightness, of course. Information, naturally. But more than anything else the facts that make the reader sit up and say "Blow me!" or "Christ Almighty!" or "Gadzooks!" as the case may be.

The old rule, known to every newspaperman, was: If a dog bites a man, that's not news; but if a man bites a dog, that is. It remains valid. It can be translated into today's intro terms:

If the Workers' Revolutionary Party denounces the Gnomes of Zurich, that's not news; if he supports them, it is.

If the Doughnut Perspex Flame Theatre Company presents a play full of four-letter words it's a yawn; if the Canterbury Cathedral Players do, it's news.

If a typist of 21 marries, who cares? But if a widow of 97 does, it's news.

If the chairman of the British Women's Total Abstinence Union stays sober her light will stay under a bushel; but if she gets pinched for drunken driving it's news.

Names, stature, jobs

This leads to another point: that more often than not it's the names that make the news. Those people whose names are constantly in the papers tend to resent it when prominence is given to things in their lives which readers may regard as unlovely. This shows a total misunderstanding of the nature of news, of the fact that the bad goes with the good.

If the daughter of a Cabinet Minister marries he will expect to have a picture of the happening in the *Daily Mail*; if her marriage breaks up within months, he must expect that to be recorded too. The two events are exact parallels: in each case the event is of no great consequence; in each case it gets into the newspaper because of the person involved.

Or, to adapt the dog truism, if my wife is bitten by a dog it won't even make the columns of the local paper, but if the Archbishop of Canterbury's wife is bitten by a dog it may well make the columns of *The Mirror*. (Its prominence, of course, might depend on which part of her collected the teeth marks). Similarly, if she reversed the official car over the Lambeth Palace cat she could expect a lot more publicity than your wife or mine would collect in similar circumstances.

The significance of names should never be overlooked in writing intros — and not merely names but positions. The importance of the event can frequently be measured by the importance or apparent importance of the individual involved.

This story is good:
Charlie Slot, 27-year-old clerk, leaped out of his car and knocked a policeman's helmet over his eyes, a court was told yesterday.

But this one is better:
Brigadier Archibald Node, leader of Britain's peace mission to Afghanistan, leaped out of his car and knocked a policeman's helmet over his eyes, a court was told yesterday.

The circumstances are exactly the same, but the story becomes better when an interesting personality becomes involved. Probably few people have ever heard of the regrettable Node, so he is not a "name" in normal usage. But he becomes a "name" because he can be identified as a brigadier and leader of the peace mission to Afghanistan, itself rather ironic.

There is also a curious way in which some *things* are more newsworthy — and therefore more intro-worthy. If the car driven by Comrade Node had been a Rolls-Royce or an Aston-Martin it would have added an air to the story which would have justified mentioning it right at the top. Likewise, while it would be quite functionless to say

who earlier had tea and cornflakes for breakfast in his Surbiton semi-detached home

something *would* be added by saying

who breakfasted at Claridge's on kippers and champagne.

A certain air of raffish high-living is introduced into the affair. Emotional reactions which could range from envy and distaste to healthy admiration are aroused, and the reader becomes personally involved.

Some occupations have what the heavy weeklies call a certain cachet. A barrister is thought by many not to be as other men. While, therefore, it is rather pointless to begin a story

Railway porter Jim Ford drove seven miles down the up-carriageway of the M1 before police caught up with him.

because the description railway porter adds nothing of great significance; it *is* worth while to begin

Barrister James de Montmorencie fforde (two smalls ffs) drove seven miles down the up-carriageway of the M1 before police caught up with him.

People don't expect an upright legal gentleman like James de Montmorencie fforde, barrister-at-law, to behave in such an unseemly fashion.

Clarity, tightness, information — and the news point that is going to start people talking. These are the qualities to seek. The intros that follow, set in bold, each hold a lesson in what ought *not* to be done. In many cases the faults overlap from one to the other. In each case I have picked out the main one.

Say that again, slowly

Marilyn Trotter, aged 28, housewife, of Pangbourne Road, New Cross, was further remanded in custody until December 9 by Mr James Cooper at Baker Road court yesterday at the request of the police when she appeared on remand charged with unlawfully and maliciously causing grievous bodily harm to Gary Albert Trotter, aged 10 months, with intent at the above address, between November 1 and November 21.

A pause to take breath. Then absorb a rule for intros: **THEY MUST BE SIMPLE, AND CAPABLE OF BEING ABSORBED AT ONE GO.**

This remarkable 65-word torrent contains the following information which is totally unnecessary to the intro:

That it was a "further remand"
That it was until December 9
The name of the magistrate

The name of the court
That the remand was at the request of the police
That she was "on remand" (second go at that)
That the alleged offence was unlawful
That it was done "with intent" (to do what?)
That it happened at an "above address"
That it happened on one of 20 or 22 days, according to how you read it.

What the intro did *not* say was that this was a story of a mother and her baby, and that the child was dead.

This is a prime example not only of missing the news but of putting so much unnecessary detail into the intro that it is highly unlikely that the reader will ever reach the meat.

Yet it could have been done so much more simply:

Gary Trotter, ten months old, died after being hit by his mother, a court was told yesterday.

She was said to have told police: "Sometimes I was vexed and angry because he would not take his feed. I slapped him about the body."

Mrs Marilyn Trotter, 28, of Pangbourne Road, New Cross, was remanded in custody at Baker Road accused of causing bodily harm.

The clutter has vanished, and a plain tale is told in a way that the simplest can absorb.

It is true that this is an extreme example, though a true one. But there often crops up a great urge to try to get too many facts in one intro:

Efforts were being made at Taunton yesterday to launch a public appeal for £6,000 for an artificial kidney machine to save the life of a local 36-year-old teacher who learned on Wednesday that without it he will probably not survive for more than a few months.

This one intro contains 13 separate facts:

1. The efforts
2. The place
3. The day
4. The appeal
5. The amount
6. The object of the exercise
7. The reason for the object
8. Another geographical reference
9. The age of the man concerned
10. His occupation
11. Another day
12. What will happen if the object is not forthcoming
13. The time in which it will happen.

All this is really too much. It's a case of 13 being unlucky for some: the readers. And it is so easy to write an intro which can be absorbed at one glance:

A 36-year-old teacher has been told that he will probably die unless £6,000 can be raised to buy an artificial kidney machine. Yesterday people in Taunton were . . .

or alternatively:

A public appeal is planned to raise £6,000 for an artificial kidney machine, needed to save the life of a 36-year-old teacher.

The complicated over-long intro tends to obscure the point that is actually being made. In this 61-word opening sentence the main news point appears in the last few words, buried not under other news points but under a recap of previous events:

In the wake of the Lincoln Cathedral verger's stink bomb revenge on the proprietor of a joke shop — he bought some stink bombs and dropped them on the shop floor in retaliation for bombs dropped in his cathedral — comes news that some pupils of the cathedral school, just round the corner, have been told the shop is now out of bounds.

The main news should be at the top where it belongs:

Some pupils at Lincoln Cathedral School have been banned from the joke shop in which the verger let off stink bombs.

It is then possible to continue with the second most important point of the story, which needs to be high up to give it balance:

But yesterday the headmaster insisted that the ban was "pure coincidence". He said boarders had been overspending there.

To bury a point such as this is to cheat and upsets many readers as well as the people concerned.

Saying it was wrong, Mr Sellers . . .

After they had found a charge using threatening words, whereby a breach of the peace was likely to be caused, proved against Peter Wilson (28), unemployed, of Riverside Drive, Calver, Bakewell Magistrates on Friday were told by Mr Leslie M Bell that the man Wilson used the threats to was a witness against him when he was before the Court earlier in the year, for being cruel to a dog.

Earlier I said that the simplest construction from the reader's point of view is The-Cat-Sat-On-The-Mat variety. The quote above, clipped from a local newspaper, demonstrates the importance of applying this rule to intros.

A newspaper might well get away with a sentence of such astonishing ugliness and obscurity if it's buried well down a story. At the start it's so likely to baffle the reader that he may well give up altogether.

Consider the obstacles. In this one sentence the reader is introduced to **THREE INDIVIDUALS** — Mr Wilson, Mr Bell (who's he?) and an anonymous witness; and a group of people — the magistrates (why the cap M?)

TWO OFFENCES — "a charge using threatening words, whereby a breach of the peace was likely to be caused" (note both the bad grammar and the acceptance of the legal jargon); and cruelty to a dog. (Why the cap C on Court?)

The reader is further confused by the fact that the two place names mentioned (Calver, Bakewell) run together; the intrusion of 14 words between "charge" and "proved"; the phrase "the man Wilson", which actually refers to two men, one of whom is being mentioned for the first time; and several lesser details.

But the main fault, which has actually led to most of the others, lies in starting the story with a subsidiary clause:

After they had found a charge . . .

From this moment the complications grow. It is inevitable that they should. The reader doesn't know who "they" are, and indeed it won't be revealed to him until 30 words later, by which time another proper noun will have intervened.

Once the subsidiary clause-main clause construction is eliminated many of the rest of the bugs disappear of their own accord:

Peter Wilson, 28, used threatening words to a man who gave evidence against him in a dog cruelty case, Bakewell magistrates were told on Friday.

Now, of course, this is not an ideal intro. It can be faulted easily. The proper course for the sub would have been to take into it information which appeared later in the story. But it has the main virtue called for in an intro: *It's easy to read.* The reason is that it is simply constructed.

A good general rule to follow: **DON'T BEGIN A STORY WITH A SUBSIDIARY CLAUSE.** And a development of the same theme: **NEVER, NEVER WRITE A NEWS INTRO STARTING WITH A PARTICIPLE.**

The participle is the weakest part of the verb. But, apart from that, the use of a participle as the first word of an intro contorts the rest of the sentence. I give only one example of the perils because this contains all that is needed:

Said to have told a detective "I did it for the experience. I am experimenting on the amount of trust between supermarkets and their customers" an Italian lawyer Fabis Massimo Benassi, 35, of Ovington Gardens, Chelsea, was fined £200 with £160 costs at Marlborough Street yesterday for shoplifting — stealing meat and cheese worth £10 while shopping in a self-service grocery store in King's Road, Chelsea.

Apart from the clutter of unnecessary detail — both things that could be said later and things that need never be said at all — consider the difficulties put in the reader's path because this story begins with a participle and a subsidiary clause. These are the problems he finds as he wades through:

Who is said to have told a store detective? And furthermore who is saying that he told what to a store detective?

Who did what for which experience?

Who is experimenting, and how did the supermarkets get into the act?

The sequence of events in the case is this:

1. A man stole from a supermarket.

2. He told a detective why.

3. He was fined.

That is also the order in which the reader can most easily absorb what happened, because it is a natural sequence. The story can be told that way:

Italian lawyer Fabis Benassi, 35, stole £10's-worth of meat and cheese from a self-service shop in King's Road, Chelsea.

He told a detective: "I did it for the experience. I am experimenting on the amount of trust between supermarkets and their customers".

Benassi, of Ovington Gardens, Chelsea, was fined £200 at Marlborough Street yesterday.

It may be that the sub wants to get "yesterday" in the first sentence, and this is certainly desirable as a general principle. This sequence is also perfectly reasonable and logical:

1. A man is fined for shoplifting.

2. Someone tells what he said.

The story could run thus:

Italian lawyer Fabis Benassi was fined £200 at Marlborough Street yesterday for stealing £10's-worth of meat and cheese from a self-service shop in King's Road, Chelsea.

Benassi, 35, of Ovington Gardens, Chelsea, told a detective: "I did it for the experience. I am experimenting on the amount of trust between supermarkets and their customers".

Or, if a shorter version is wanted:

Italian lawyer Fabis Benassi, of Ovington Gardens, Chelsea, was fined £200 for shoplifting at Marlborough Street yesterday. He told a detective: "I am experimenting on the amount of trust between supermarkets and their customers".

Each of these forms is simple, direct, and avoids any kind of inversion. Intros are better that way.

What, all at once?

Salvage experts are today deciding whether to attempt to raise the 80-year-old paddle steamer *Totnes Castle* which sank in Bigbury Bay, Devon, as she was being towed from Dartmouth, Devon, where she had been used on pleasure trips up the River Dart, to Plymouth, where she was to be broken up, at the weekend.

Some intros begin directly enough, and then get lost in a maze of subsidiary clauses. The one above is a good example. From an intro point of view the steamer is adequately placed by the clause "which sank in Bigbury Bay, Devon". The sentence could reasonably end there. But the reporter, apparently determined to give the reader indigestion, goes on:

as she was being towed . . .

Where she had been used . . .

where she was to be broken up . . .

It is unnecessary. The sentence demonstrates the virtue of the full stop, the greatest aid to simple English ever invented. Even without rewriting or recasting the intro can be improved enormously:

Salvage experts are today deciding whether to try to raise the 80-year-old paddle steamer 'Totness Castle', which sank in Bigbury Bay, Devon, at the weekend.

The steamer was being towed from Dartmouth, where she was used on pleasure trips, to Plymouth to be broken up.

Almost as bad as the practice of stuffing an intro with defining or descriptive clauses is the use of a succession of prepositional phrases.

As bonfires blazed in Barnstaple last night, from India came news to an 11-year-old boy of an event to remind him of a scene in earlier days which . . .

Sentences like this must be rebuilt so that the reader does not have to climb over prepositions to get to the point.

Sorry, I'm not with you

There were hopes yesterday that most of the 550 workers expected to be made redundant will have found new jobs before GEC close the London headquarters of AEI next March.

Another important rule for writing intros is this: **NEVER INTRODUCE UNIDENTIFIED FACTS OR PEOPLE OR EVENTS.** The intro above provides an example of a faulty construction which does just this. It is not an outstandingly bad one, but it is one which will cause many readers to pause momentarily to work it out.

The first part of the sentence says:

There were hopes yesterday that most of the 550 workers expected to be made redundant will have found new jobs . . .

The snag here is that the workers are unidentified. The reader simply doesn't know who is being talked about. He then reads on:

. . . before GEC close the London headquarters of AEI next March.

At this point he has to work it out for himself. He has to assume that the 550 will lose their jobs because of the closure, although this is not spelt out. This arises because of a simple constructional fault. It is necessary to link the sackings and the closure immediately:

Most of the 550 workers expected to be sacked before the London headquarters of Associated Electrical Industries closes down are likely to find new jobs.

Immediately the reader knows which lot of workers is being talked about, and that is as it should be.

This quote is an example of a different kind of confusion caused by bad construction:

Police in Sussex yesterday stepped up their hunt for a man who assaulted an 11-year-old boy a fortnight ago after threatening him with a knife, following a fresh attack on a young woman.

It only becomes clear who is attacking who and in what order in the second paragraph:

A Gurkha knife with a curved 6-inch blade was used in the attack on the woman, Mrs Amanda Smith, of Haslingden, Lancashire. Police think the two incidents may be linked.

THE NEWS is that a woman has been attacked.

AN ADDITIONAL POINT is that the attack may be linked with an earlier one.

And that is the way it should be done:

A man with a curved Gurkha knife attacked Mrs Amanda Smith, 21-year-old mother of three, as she walked along a cliff-top path.

Police think the attack may be linked with one on a boy of 11 a fortnight ago.

If, on the other hand, the story is a follow-up (and only the careful placing of the word *yesterday* might imply that) it can be simplified like this:

Police suspect a link between an attack with a Gurkha knife on a young woman and an earlier assault on an 11-year-old boy.

Either way is direct and suited to the facts.

And NUTS to you, too

TUC leaders may be asked to intervene in the clash between the NUT and the NAS over the new pay structure proposed by the ILEA.

I have dealt earlier with obstructions set in the way of the reader by the use of sets of initials. The point becomes even more important in the writing of intros.

An abbreviation of this kind is rarely justified in an opening par. Somebody, somewhere, may not know what it means. Somebody else, somewhere else, is going to momentarily slow up while he works out what it means.

Of course there are exceptions. No doubt TUC is one of them. But I suggest that if you threw the initials NUT at the first 100 workers leaving the night shift at Ford's there would be an uncomfortably high number of don't knows. Try them on NAS or ILEA and even more would be disconcerted.

A good rule: **DON'T USE THIS KIND OF ABBREVIATION IN YOUR INTRO UNLESS YOU'RE ABSOLUTELY SURE YOUR READERS WILL KNOW WHAT YOU'RE ON ABOUT.**

All the time spell it out, or define it, or get rid of it altogether. It is bearable to say:

Three hundred thousand members of the National and Local Government Officers Association are demanding a 20 per cent pay rise.

But it is more exciting and human and (to use an in-word) emotive to write:

Three hundred thousand Town Hall workers, from town clerks to tea boys, are demanding a 20p-in-the-£ pay rise.

The purists may protest that 703 or 2,703 of Nalgo's members have no connection with town halls, but the intro represents a broad truth in a way the average reader will understand.

An additional point here is that it is important not to *begin* a story with a set of initials. There are two reasons for this:

1. If the newspaper's style is to begin with drop letters the result will be extremely ugly, particularly if the old-fashioned practice of full points in abbreviations is followed:

N.A.L.G.O. is to demand a 20p in-the-£ rise for its 300,000 members, who work in town halls all over Britain.

2. This is by far the more important — the use of abbreviations at the start of the story will slow up the rate at which the reader will absorb the story — *even if he can translate them instantly.* A simple, readily-recognisable set of initials like TUC is jarring, because it uses a kind of shorthand. The initial impact is of three words — Tee-You-See — concentrated in a couple of ems.

Is that one I missed?

Firemen with breathing apparatus were early today searching the smoking debris of Tiplady's department store, for possible further victims, after yesterday afternoon's blaze in which seven people are known to have died.

A constant and understandable urge among sub-editors on daily newspapers is to throw forward stories to some point beyond that reached by the evening papers and television.

In many cases the urge is a mistaken one. If followed it frequently has two results:

1. The main point of the story becomes obscured by a mass of words.

2. The construction of the intro tends to clumsiness.

It is wrong to assume that everyone has spent the previous night reading the evening papers or watching television. It is also wrong to assume that if they *have* briefly heard of a murder or a fire or a *coup d'etat* they want it to appear in disguise the following day.

What they do want, and what they should get, is a crisper, better-written story, filled with more interesting detail and supplementing what has been written or said earlier. Far better for the story above to have read:

Fire swept Tiplady's department store yesterday. By early today, with firemen still searching the smoking ruins, the death toll had reached seven.

Or alternatively:

Seven people are now known to have died in the fire which swept Tiplady's department store yesterday. Firemen searching the smoking ruins early today feared that the final toll may be still higher.

This is not an argument against the genuine throw-forward. If an event about which most people are likely to know has an important sequel then that can be the intro. What I am arguing against is the *contrived* throw-forward. This is the formula under which every murder happening before 7 pm has a Lowest Common Denominator intro by the following morning:

Police of four counties were early today hunting the brutal killer of . . .

Or:

Detectives with tracker dogs combed wasteland last night in their search for the gentle killer of . . .

Instead of:

A girl with a bikini-shaped golden tan was hacked to death yesterday in a woodland glade known as Lover's Lay. Last night police . . .

Even in the case of the genuine throw-forward there is a lot to be said for the direct approach combined with the "what happens now?" touch. Suppose the Chancellor of the Exchequer resigns at 5 pm one dismal evening. The complete throw-forward begins:

Mr John Blank, who resigned as Chancellor of the Exchequer last night, is expected to take up one of several offers from industry.

This is fair enough. But there is still a case for being more direct, even if only for the benefit of those out of touch, and saying:

Mr John Blank resigned as Chancellor of the Exchequer last night — and was immediately offered several big-business posts.

The first style smacks of compromise. The second, at any rate, makes it clear what the big news is. If the sub is convinced that nowhere on God's Earth is there anyone not privy to this Great Drama he can at least display his decisiveness by saying:

Mr John Blank was last night offered several big-business jobs within hours of his quitting as Chancellor of the Exchequer.

The rule for throw-forwards is really quite simple: **IF IT'S REALLY ADVANCED, GO FOR IT DIRECTLY. IF IT'S NOT, DON'T GET MIXED UP IN A MESSY COMPROMSIE.**

English unofficial prose

The Housing and Public Works Committee of Oswald-twistle Urban District Council decided at its meeting on Wednesday to make a formal approach to the Accrington branch of the Transport and General Workers' Union with regard to delays in the provision of an Accrington Transport Department bus service to its new housing development off Leningrad Mill Street.

Well, you could hardly have a more formal approach than, that. It serves to demonstrate the dangers of official bodies taking over intros. There are probably few more depressing words in the English language than *Oswaldtwistle Urban District Council*, but nine of them are certainly *Accrington branch of the Transport and General Workers' Union.*

There is no doubt that, with rare exceptions, the intrusion of an official or semi-official body into an opening sentence tends to cast a blight on the rest of the proceedings. There are two ways in which their dampening effect can be lessened:

1. Keep them out of the first par altogether.

2. When they do rear their ugly heads reduce them to as great a state of informality as is consistent with good sense — "Oswaldtwistle Council's housing committee" rather than "the Housing and Public Works Committee of Oswaldtwistle Urban District Council".

In most cases it does not require any great effort. It is easy to say:

Members of the Booksellers, Stationers and Hard Back Distributors Association last night welcomed the decision by Blankton Press to increase their profit on sales by five per cent.

But it is not much more difficult, and certainly it is more appetising from the point of view of the general reader, to say:

Ten thousand booksellers last night welcomed the decision by one of Britain's biggest educational publishers to up their profits by 10p in the £.

The name of the outfit, and of the publishers, can be kept till later.

It happened in Blockley — so what?

Blockley, Lancashire, branch of the Young Conservatives, have shocked members of the party by holding a "rugby" sing-song at which four-letter words were bandied about.

That's a good story, by any sort of measuring stick. But the question is: Should the sub have put the place name in the first paragraph? Or if it was already in, should he have left it there?

The answer is bound to be of the yes-if-no-unless variety. Basically it depends on the market. IF the place name attracts more readers than it puts off then there is a case for having it in the intro. If it doesn't it should be left out.

The story above might have appeared in three types of newspaper:

1. A local paper circulating in Blockley and its immediate surroundings. Here it will probably be left in, because Blockley people are clearly more interested in Blockley Young Tories than in any other variety.

2. An evening paper which includes Blockley in its circulation area. Here it depends on how well Blockley is known (do a lot of people in the circulation area go shopping there?) to the readers considered as a whole. If Blockley is a big, significant place then there is an argument for keeping the name in. But if the reaction is going to be "Who cares about Blockley?" (or even worse "Has anybody ever heard of Blockley?") it is better buried further down the story. The Lancashire interest can, of course, be retained:

A sing-song at which four-letter words were used by Lancashire Young Conservatives has shocked older members of the party.

This way the non-Blockleyites are more inclined to read on, some with ever-mounting tension at the thought that their own dear young ones might be involved.

3. All papers outside the circulation area, whether evening or morning. Here there is no case at all for including the place name in the first sentence. To do so only discourages the reader. "Blockley, Lancashire" are killing words not only in Christchurch, Hants, but also in Malpas, Cheshire. The intro should be completely delocalised:

A young Conservative sing-song at which four-letter words were used has shocked older members of the party.

There is one major exception to these rules: **IF THE PLACE NAME ITSELF IS SPECIALLY WELL KNOWN OR SIGNIFICANT IT IS WORTH PUTTING IN THE FIRST PAR.**

It is obviously daft to say:

A city is to take over control of all transport services within its boundaries. when by city is meant Greater London.

Likewise it is desirable to begin

Blackpool Tower fell down last night . . .

Southend Pier blew up last night . . .

The names of all major seaside towns are newsworthy. They defy the rules about place names.

There is also an argument for putting a place name in an intro if it seems funny or peculiar in relation to a set of circumstances. Some place names are, unfortunately for the people who live there, regarded as comic. But this does not mean there is any virtue in beginning a story:

People in Tintwistle, Cheshire, are in revolt against a plan to build seven new pubs in the main street.

A touch of the off-beat is needed:

The Bottoms of Tintwistle are on the march. Twenty-seven people called Bottom, all living in or just outside the village, are in revolt against a plan to rename a street Black Side.

or —

Old Frank Hearthrug, the Sage of Elmers End, yesterday called off his boycott of the local post office.

The place name must not only be part of the intro; it must also be *seen* to be part of it.

What's that got to do with it?

Fred Slopstone, 17-year-old motor mechanic, of Cheyne Walk, Penge, SE, was jailed for 42 years at the Old Bailey yesterday, on 13 charges of robbing post offices in Peckham between 1980 and 1984 and stealing money, postal orders, savings stamps and national insurance stamps to a total value of £798,428.98

That is an invention. I like to believe that no one — or, at least, no one who has passed through the National Council training scheme — would ever perpetuate such an intro; but I've seen some that come pretty near it.

The point is that it is packed from orifice to breakfast-time with the kind of technical detail that has no part in an intro. It is not necessary for the reader to know in the first par:

That Fred is a mechanic;

That he lives where he does (at any rate in such detail);

The number of charges;

The situation of the post offices;

The dates of the offences; or

The details of the goodies.

The *intro-type* facts left are that Fred Slopstone, an infant in law, had spent four years of his infancy nicking things from post offices, and got nearly £800,000 and 42 years' jail for his pains.

These things alone are enough. Or it may be that there are other relevant or exciting details worth introducing into the first par. Comrade Slopstone may be an Old Etonian gone wrong, or the son of a former President of the Board of Trade. He may only recently have become a mechanic after gaining 11 A-levels. He may have the highest IQ in Mensa. Any of these things could be worth saying right at the start by way of a bit of colour, because they are either germane or intriguing. But the sheer technical details should be buried.

Beware also of cluttering up intros with irrelevant details that add nothing. It is fair enough to say:

A mother of four was jailed for two years for shoplifting yesterday

because the presence of four kids introduces new elements into the jailing (Who'll look after them? Is the sentence too severe in the context?)

But it serves no useful purpose to say:

A father of four was appointed head of Britain's world-beating nuclear power industry yesterday

because the kids are a functionless detail that falls naturally further down the story. The reader here needs to know whether he is 27 or 63; whether he is a former managing director of Ford's or whether he started life as a reporter; whether he is a scientific genius or a business whizz-kid or a political hack who is likely to let the whole industry fall to bits as a result of ineptitude rather than malice.

There is a real danger in the kind of intro which is packed with irrelevancies: that the things that matter are excluded. Take this genuine, word-for-word example of the opening paragraph of a reporter's story:

Evidence for the defence was heard by Mr John Aubrey-Fletcher at Marlborough Street court in a case in which five persons face charges resulting from a demonstration in King's Road, Chelsea, on 30th October to protest against the sentence passed on Brian Jones of the Rolling Stones. The five were then further remanded on bail for two days. They strongly deny the allegations.

The sub needs to ask these questions, all directly related to the matter of unnecessary technical details:

WHY is evidence for the defence introduced at this stage?

WHO CARES about Mr John Aubrey-Fletcher, and who is he anyway?

DOES the name of the court matter in the first par?

HAS THE DATE really anything to do with the event?

DOES IT MATTER, from an intro point of view, whether they were remanded on bail or in the nick, or whether it was for two days or three, or whether they deny it or admit it?

All these points are, in fact, extraneous to the intro. But it is interesting to see what they exclude. The intro doesn't say that the five included Mick Jagger's brother, Susie Creamcheese (born Susan Zeiger) the "professional demonstrator", or the chap who wrote the ad in *The Times* calling for the legalisation of cannabis. It doesn't seize on any of the intriguing points in the story that followed.

There are many ways of dealing with the story. One subbed version began like this:

DANCER Susan Zeiger — stage name Susie Creamcheese — said yesterday that she heard policemen and women "sniggering" about her after she was arrested during a demonstration against the jail sentence on Rolling Stone Brian Jones.

Zeiger, 20, known as the "Queen of the Hippies", said that she was put in a cell at Chelsea Police Station.

She overheard police officers outside joking and saying: "Susie Creamcheese, professional demonstrator."

There are a dozen other possible intros, all capable of getting the reader interested. But that on the original copy is certainly not one of them.

That's interesting — who said it?

"I found their way of life exceptionally interesting from the point of view of my own profession" said Mrs Joanna Pauker, the sexologist, at Heathrow Airport yesterday, when she returned from a visit to the "hippie" areas of San Francisco

For those who have noted the earlier section on reporting speeches little more need be said about stories beginning with quotes.

The almost-unbreakable rule (nothing in this job is *completely* without exception) that the reader must first know who is speaking applies not only to speeches and formal interviews.

The example above demonstrates the confusion that can be caused. It is not merely that 99.9 per cent of quotes are valueless until we know who is speaking. In this case we have introduced these unidentified trying objects:

> *I*
>
> *their*
>
> *my*

Only *after* the quote is over is the reader able to work out what the I-their-my bit is all about.

I suggest this rule: when you've finally convinced yourself that you've got a story that needs a quote start — have another go. You'll probably find a better intro.

Wake me up when you've done

All her life Miss Minnie Birtwistle has been interested in the problems of children from broken homes. Living alone with her three cats, she has had time to consider the way in which . . .

Need I go on? This form of intro — the delayed drop, the slow burn — is the most difficult one to practice. It assumes that the story is so beautifully written, so compulsively readable, that the customer will be swept along till he reaches a buried news point 12 paragraphs on.

But life is not like that. The average newspaper reader does not approach his paper as he does a short story: it is quite likely that he is reading it standing in a bus or in the 4½ minutes he's waiting for a train. The incidental facts are probably not vivid enough to carry him through to the climax.

Can he, in the case above, be expected to plod through even half-a-dozen paragraphs about Miss Birtwistle and her sociological interests before reaching the action? It is not much more likely that his attention would be gripped by starting with the hard stuff:

Social worker Minnie Birtwistle — the Angel of Islington — was battered to death on the steps of a Salvation Army mission last night by a boy she had befriended.

The boy, 17-year-old Clive Cornet, shot himself through the head as . . .

All this is not to say that delayed drop stories are out. But 99 times out of a hundred the news is the thing.

Excuse me while I throw up

Smells from the dry closets in Bugsworth and the nuisance from flies were mentioned at the meeting of Chapel-Tidmarsh rural council on Wednesday.

That is a version of an intro I read in a local paper, toned down because even with books one should consider readers with delicate stomachs. It is more important still in newspapers.

Never give a reader filth for breakfast. Never repel him (or more likely her) with an excess of blood or messy detail. If it's necessary to the story — bury it.

It's one thing to imply gently that a 16-year-old blonde — "She was a quiet, homeloving girl" friends said — has been done to death in a nasty way. It's quite another to say in the first sentence that she's been disembowelled with a rusty carving knife.

Those with a taste for this kind of thing are amply catered for by a certain kind of book shop. Most newspaper readers are likely to experience revulsion rather than stimulation.

Closets and cornflakes make uncomfortable partners at breakfast.

Masked hatchet-men last night . . .

Almost the last word on intros, put into my mind by a former Chief Sub:
ALWAYS TRY TO MAKE THE FIRST WORD DO SOME WORK.

It's surprising how often an intro can be improved by making sure the first word is a strong one.

And definitely the last word . . .

. . . in intros. If anyone can find a more excrutiating, unintelligible opening sentence than the following, reproduced here in its full original stereophonic horror, I will substitute it in the sixth edition of this book:

Johan van Jaarsveld, scriptwriter/actor (author of "Verspeelde Lente"), speaking with Clarence Keyter in an edition of "Verslag" which suggested social censorship as a viable alternative to our heavily State controlled form of publications control, with reference to the Act as a protection against the threat to Afrikaner identity: "I think it's a myth that we (Afrikaners) must be protected. If we have such a shallow society, if our heritage lies so shallow, is it worth protecting it by legislation?"

And to make it worse, in the page it made 25 lines of 10 pt across 8 ems!

In the celebrated words of a former night editor of *The Mirror:* "What xxxx subbed that?"

If you want to get ahead, get a headline

A newspaper headline has many functions, but one of them overshadows all the others: **IT MUST MAKE THE CUSTOMER WANT TO READ THE STORY BELOW.**

This is fundamentally what a headline is about. Every other rule in this chapter is made to be broken if breaking it results in a best-selling headline. It's a good thing in a headline:

> *To tell the news*
> *To use active verbs*
> *To phrase line by line*
> *To avoid jargon*

and a lot of other things. But it's not vital. It's highly unlikely that a newsless, verbless, badly-phrasing, jargon-full headline would force the reader to read on. But if one cropped up that did — that's the headline that's wanted.

Is it possible to suggest any characteristics common to read-me headlines? I think it is.

1. They are vigorous and idiomatic. The stilted multi-deck headline never sold any story.

2. They stimulate an emotional reaction from the reader; they make him feel involved in the story.

3. They bear a relation to the market involved. With some newspapers this is easy. If the *News of the World* carries a headline saying "The day the kitchen door swung open" the customer knows automatically that he's faced with a story about a Baptist lay preacher crashing in on a pattern maker's wife in her trim council house with lust in his heart and a pound note in his hand.

There are, of course, headlines which are tailor-made for any market.

The one that says:

PRINCESS DIANA: A STATEMENT

would sell the *Financial Times* although the customers may feel a trifle let down when it's merely an announcement that she's got a boil on her bottom.

A good headline writer is a valuable member of any subs' table. For one thing he saves the chief sub so much trouble. In ten years of chief subbing I found that one of the most niggling things was having to stop headlines on the way to the Printer, and keep them on my desk until I had time to think of one myself. The situation was occasionally made worse by my writing the head on a point the sub had cut from the story. This may not have indicated that the sub had cut something of inherent worth, but it did indicate that he had cut some point *on which it was possible to sell the story to the reader.*

This leads me to make a suggestion of a certain nature — and I feel bound to call it that because many old hands will regard it as so outrageous as to be indecent:

WRITE THE HEADING FIRST.

It is a practice I followed for many years as a sub. But, much more relevant, it is done every day by back-benchers and chief subs everywhere, who write heads on page leads and picture spreads even before giving out the copy.

The results are good not only because the headings are written by experienced headline-writers, but by the order of events: The selling-point is found first, and things proceed from there.

If the system works for the executives why shouldn't it work for the subs? My own experience is that with a headline in mind the story falls into place all that more easily. And it's surprising how often the phrase or point that seems unnecessary in the subbing process can provide (or at any rate improve on) a heading.

A sub coming fresh to national news stories can improve his own technique by studying how the other papers have handled the headlines on stories he's done. If one of them catches his eye it is worth his while to analyse why.

So much for the general principles. In the rest of this chapter I have set down some of the guidelines that help a sub to write good headlines. They *are* guidelines and not rules. They are broken every day, and often with very good reason.

Each section is prefaced by two headings, one good and one not so good, each illustrating a point.

Maggie says No again

Britain's "No" on "Green" £

In these two headlines, three lessons.

No. 1. USE THE ACTIVE VOICE WHERE YOU CAN.

There's nothing quite like it for strengthening a head. "MP urges Premier to quit" is a better heading than "Resign call by MP". And "Mystery blonde shot in wood" is better than "Mystery of shot blonde in wood".

One qualification: Avoid the word WAS. This, unlike the active verbs, slows down and weakens the head. In many cases it has the strange effect of making it seem *un*newsy and even faintly historical. "Man on beach was ex-vicar" can be much better rendered as "Ex-vicar named as man on beach".

No. 2. AVOID A CLUTTER OF PUNCTUATION.

The first heading is entirely free of it and yet quite clear (the cap N in No sees to that). The second has an apostrophe and two sets of quotes — the first set pedantic and the second apologetic.

Straight news headings should, as far as possible, be written so that punctuation is *unnecessary*. The one simple phrase that trips off the tongue without pause is the aim. A comma means a two-part headline, which is slower. Quote marks, occasionally necessary for legal reasons, often indicate a separate thought coming up. Exclamation marks are sometimes a confession of failure, a signal to the reader saying "Look how clever or stimulating or witty or sensational this is!!!" Question marks, except in special circumstances, are to be avoided because the newspaper's business is telling people, not asking them.

All this, of course, refers to straight headlines. In the gimmick headline punctuation can be used for dramatic effect. Even full stops are OK. There is nothing wrong with this on a picture of a pop-star in the making

This girl is 4 ft 3 in tall. By next week she'll be something big in show business. When you hear her voice you'll understand why.

In this kind of presentation even the neglected colon can come back into its own.

No. 3. PERSONALISE WHERE YOU CAN.

In the first headline an immediate image is created by naming Maggie as the guilty party. In the second the much less evocative "Britain" is used, and the headline loses by it.

This is an obvious case, the principle can be applied more widely. GADDAFI is often better than LIBYA. And headlines often gain by pinning it on Reagan rather than on the U.S.

In official matters, too, the use of the name of the individual rather than the department can help to bring the headline to life. A Minister's name— or better still his nickname — is better if it's well known than the name of the Ministry.

TEBBIT TO SEE NO-JOB MEN

Grey area delegates will see PM on jobs, new industry

Three points arising out of these headings.

No. 1. AVOID CRAMMING IN TOO MUCH INFORMATION.

The first is simple, direct, and unwordy, but contains the essential germ of the story. The second has so much information packed into it that it's difficult to absorb at one go:

> *The delegates*
> *Where they're from*
> *Who they're seeing*
> *The TWO subjects under discussion*

One local paper I know not only makes a habit of doing its main splash heading on these lines, but precedes it with an even more complex strapline, and an almost equally wordy second deck. Frequently the story underneath is almost unnecessary except for the connoisseurs of jargon and officialese.

A good rule is: Decide your main point, and stick to it.

No. 2. AVOID ABBREVIATIONS IF YOU CAN.

It is true that some abbreviations are bearable, and indeed even virtuous, in headlines. TV and BBC, for example, are so much part of the language that any objection on aesthetic grounds fail before the case begins to be made. TUC can survive. There are others. But largely speaking an attempt should be made to avoid abbreviations on the twin grounds of ugliness and unintelligibility.

"Railmen threaten national strike" is better than "NUR threaten national strike", Come to that "Loco men threaten national strike" is better than "ASLEF threaten national strike".

Why say "NUM", which sounds like a Moscow department store, in a heading when you can say "miners"? If you do, some section of the population will be baffled and bemused. Why say "NUT" when a word everybody knows — teachers — is available?

A good rule: never use a set of initials if you can find an ordinary English word that will do the job.

No. 3. A COMMA IS NOT A SUBSTITUTE FOR A WORD.

In the second headline, the comma between "jobs" and "new industry" is standing in for the word "and". The effect is to slow it up and spoil the flow of words. It also literally makes it unspeakable, in the sense that it can't be spoken aloud without an unnatural effect.

Some newspapers ban completely the substitution of a comma for "and", and a good thing too.

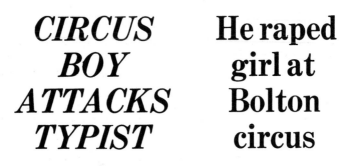

Four lessons in these headings.

No. 1. AVOID THE ANONYMOUS HE, SHE, AND THEY.

Words which introduce unidentified people are an irritation to the reader. They pose an unfair question: Who the hell is *he* anyway? They are also boring, because they are vague, cardboardy figures.

There are many devices a sub can use to avoid this weakening practice. Occupations are one: LAWYER FOUND DRUNK AFTER PARTY is better than HE WAS DRUNK AFTER LAWYER'S PARTY. Ages can be useful: DOG SAVES MAN OF 82 FROM DROWNING is an improvement on DOG SAVES HIM FROM DROWNING IN POND.

Any kind of status description can be employed: WIDOW KILLED IN FALL FROM TRICYCLE rather than HER TRICYCLE GOT OUT OF CONTROL.

Then, if all else fails, there is the device employed in the first heading — the simple transference of the situation to the subject, so that the boy visiting the circus becomes CIRCUS BOY. If the man at the party had been something unappealing like a sewage farm shoveller instead of a lawyer he could have become PARTY MAN. The old chap in the pond could be DOG-LOVER, the mad cyclist TRICYCLE WIDOW.

The sub should never overlook the use of names in this connection. Many a difficulty has been overcome by calling somebody OLD FRED or AUNT MAY. And, of course, some names like Custard and Shed and Pudding demand to be put in headlines, particularly if the facts of the story provide a happy juxtaposition:

Mr BOOZER HAD ONE OVER THE EIGHT.

Or one I remember on a story about a private eye called Lightning:

Mr LIGHTNING STRIKES AT THREE.

Whichever way it's done, avoid the unidentified *he, she* and *they*.

No. 2. BE CAREFUL WITH WORDS SUCH AS BUM

In these enlightened days they're all right in the text, but there are still a lot of people around who are offended by such extreme directness.

Subs may regard them as hypersensitive or even squeamish, but they are the people who are actually paying their pennies for the paper while the sub is getting his for free. In the end it comes down to what kind of story it is — and, even more important, what kind of newspaper you're working for.

One newspaper peer would not allow the word adultery in his newspapers at all, which I think is carrying things too far. But there *are* limits, and they are governed by the kind of readership.

No. 3. AVOID THE PAST TENSE WHEN POSSIBLE.

The active present is preferable all the time. I know that occasionally the past tense is unavoidable on stories from the courts or inquests. But even here it can often be avoided simply by varying the angle of the headline.

The only past-tense heading that really works is that in which a death is stated or implied, usually in an emotive kind of way:

CHARLIE THE WATCHMAN DIED FOR HIS DOG
OLD TOM LOVED HIS DOG TOO WELL
CHAMPION CYCLIST FOUGHT TO THE LAST

But rather than VICAR DRANK TOO MUCH, always go for 10-PINT VICAR FINED or PUB-CRAWL PARSON SAYS: SORRY I WAS SLOSHED.

Final lesson:

No. 4. AVOID PLACE NAMES UNLESS THEY'RE DOING A JOB.

This rule does not apply to purely local papers. There the principle dealt with under intros applies. But in newspapers of wider circulation no place name should appear in a heading unless it fulfils a useful purpose. Thus in:

LONDON BRIDGE IS COMING DOWN

the word London is vital. Equally in:

SOUTHEND PIER ABLAZE

the word Southend can be justified on the grounds that this pier is one of the famous in the land and millions of people have tramped over it at some time or another. The use of M1 in

FOUR DIE IN M1 PILE-UP

can be supported on the same grounds. But

FOUR DIE IN LUTON CRASH

is no use for anywhere except the Luton area. More people will be put off by "Luton" than attracted by it. In Hampstead they'll all fall off their chairs with yawning and switch on the Third Programme.

Cut-back in houses programme urged

Demands a cut in housing programme

Two faults to note in the second headline.

No. 1. NEVER USE A VERB WITHOUT ITS SUBJECT.

This ugly American practice is mercifully rarely seen in national newspapers in this country, but some local papers have fallen prey to it. It is unfair on the reader, because like the unidentified "he" it poses a question not answered in the heading. *Who* is demanding the cut in the housing programme? The first heading doesn't provide an answer either: it doesn't need to because it doesn't pose a question. But the question screams out from the second.

The no-subject style is also undesirable because it *sounds* unnatural. People may leave the verb to be assumed in ordinary speech, but they never leave out the subject.

No. 2. AVOID ENDING LINES WITH INEFFECTIVES.

Headings are read line by line, and the more they phrase line by line the easier they are to absorb. Thus it is better to write

VICAR HITS WIFE
WITH MALLET

than it is to say

VICAR'S WIFE HURT IN
MALLET ATTACK

The top line of the first heading makes sense on its own because it represents a complete thought. The top line of the second stops halfway through the thought. It can easily be improved by turning over the word "in" and filling out the top line:

WIFE OF VICAR HURT
IN MALLET ATTACK

Of course it's not possible to do this all the time, particularly in single column headings with a count of 5½ letters and spaces. But it is an ideal to be strived for. And it is a good thing to resolve never to commit these offences against readability:

1. Ending a line, even in a single column heading, with the indefinite article. Notice how the 'a' in "Demands a" jars when it is read line by line.

2. Failing to make the top line of a turning banner stand on its own. If the top line is across seven columns and the second is across three the top line is absorbed first. So

Mini-skirt girls attacked
by Beatles

registers more quickly than

Beatles attack girls in mini-skirts

With this the eye stops momentarily at "in" and then has to move back several columns before normal sense is resumed.

UNIONS OPPOSE SCHOOL CUTS

BID TO SLASH SCHOOLS RAPPED

Only one comment here:

BEWARE OF HEADLINE JARGON.

There are some words which demand to be put in headlines. They are short, terse, and make the point exactly. Such are *bid*, *slash*, and *rapped* in the headline above.

But there is a danger here. Words such as quit, probe, move, plea, rush, cut, ban, dash, slash, crash, quiz and hits are so useful that they tend to be overworked. They become part of the lazy sub's armoury. Instead of being kept for the occasion when no other word will do the job, they are used out of habit, so that the paper is filled to overflowing with them.

It's an act of madness for any editor to ban the word *Red*, as a now-defunct editor of a now-defunct newspaper did. But like the other jargon words it should be used with restraint.

Premier must go says MP

Time to change Premier

—MP

One simple, three-word lesson:

DON'T USE TAGLINES.

They are pathetic, apologetic little things, abortions caused by idleness. They are typographically ugly and verbally unsatisfactory. In the example above the tag "—MP" should be part of the main heading, which has no significance without it.

Taglines mainly creep in on court stories, where the sub finds it difficult to qualify a statement without one:

MAN SHOT MISTRESS IN STOMACH
—magistrates told

It is often a struggle to avoid this kind of tag, but struggle is good for the soul. One possible way out is to use a statement that won't be disputed:

BACHELOR-FLAT GIRL SHOT IN STOMACH

Another is to get the qualification in the main deck:

MAN SHOT MISTRESS IN BED, COURT TOLD

With this kind of story chief-subs sometimes make the task impossible by giving out complicated court stories with headings that have a count of five letters to the line. It's their fault that they get lousy headings back, and the only comfort is that such chief subs are dying out.

In these circumstances the only thing the man on the desk can do is to keep his determination to avoid taglines. Or at any rate avoid the extremes of the incredible Charlie Rigby, who while a sub on the *News Chronicle* put a 12 point tagline on a 72 point splash banner. *He* had an excuse: he was writing his book on sub-editing at the time.

Julie Christie hit by scooter

Scooter man in row with actress

Rule for straplines:

WRITE THEM LAST.

The reason is simple. The eye is caught first by the main deck. It must therefore be completely self-contained and be based on the main point of the story. The way to do this is to write it as though the strapline didn't exist — and then use the strap to add a point.

Most straps are there for some typographical reason, such as linking a picture with a story. It is quite likely that the reader will get enough from the main deck and not read the strap at all.

The sub, therefore, should ban completely any main deck which is *dependent* on a strap, except, of course, where the strap is merely a legal get-out. He should particularly avoid those that assume, and wrongly, that the strap is read first — those that end in "and . . . ", "so . . . " and "then . . . ".

The 14 bigamous wives of Hamish McToe

Railway porter 'married' fourteen times

These two headings make one point:

SOMETIMES THE LABEL IS BEST.

Most newspapers have a down on label headlines, and rightly. Unless they're discouraged they tend to spread lazily through every page. But a *good* label can sell a story, and is better than a mediocre active heading.

On the day after a South African surgeon performed the world's first heart transplant the splash heading in *The Mirror* said:

THE HEART THAT KNOWS NO COLOUR BAR

And in the *Mail:*

THE HEART THAT BEATS BEYOND A COLOUR BAR

And in the *Express:*

THE HEART THAT BEAT APARTHEID

You could hardly have better authority than that. But: watch them. They need to be good. A rash of headings beginning "The day . . ." usually results in a complete ban, which is a pity.

The caption's your chance for creation

THE good caption writer is rare and therefore prized. There are many subs who can competently handle a running story, or knock up a passable page lead from a PA law report, or do a crisp nibs column; but there are far fewer who can create a superb caption.

The word "create" is chosen deliberately, for caption writing, more than anything else the sub is asked to do, can be an act of creation. With most jobs the sub is improving on someone else's work: assembling the facts in a more logical order, cutting, polishing, providing a new nose that is more likely to tempt the customer to read on. Even when he is doing a complete rewrite he is working on material provided by someone else.

But the self-contained story caption is different. Here the sub can let his own creative skill take command, and from virtually no material produce a gem. The essential element is imagination. I knew one absolutely first-class sub who had a complete blank on captions: the moment he was faced with a picture, the imagination he showed in other fields just vanished. Given a picture of, say, an old working-class rebel taking his seat in the House of Lords, he would ask, quite sincerely:

What is there to say except "Ted Hill, the former trade union leader, arriving at the House of Lords to take his seat yesterday"?

There is a great deal more to say. The sub with a caption-orientated mind will find an actual pleasure in looking at a picture like this, and immediately start thinking of the words he will use to enable the reader to share it. He will play on the splendid irony of the situation: this representative of the antediluvian trade union left, this Terrible Ted of the TUC, now embraced by an outfit even more outdated. He will bring out the contrasts: the Stately House and the working class home; the before and after. He will check if Ted has ever uttered any derogatory words about the House of Lords, and so on. In this way he will provide the imagination the reader lacks.

Give them something extra

There is one key question to ask about a self-contained caption: Does it ADD to the picture? If it does, it's on the way to success. It is never enough to *describe* the picture, for the reader has eyes of his own.

TO SAY that Mr Edward Heath was wearing a double-breasted suit borders on the fatuous, but to work in the point that it cost him £1000 and has cloth-covered buttons is worth while.

TO SAY that Mr Arthur Scargill's hair was tousled is to state the obvious, but to mention that only two days earlier he'd had it styled by Princess Diana's hairdresser* provides a little zest.

These are the simple things, but caption-writing is more than just this. In its highest form it consists of taking a picture which pictorially is of little merit and so dealing out the words that the whole assumes an intrinsic value.

Let me take one example — from the *Sun*, a newspaper which is splendid on captions. The picture is quite dreary in itself: King Constantine and his family arriving in Rome in his private plane. You might call it historic but dull, and the eye passes over it as it does with historic events. But note the way that the words bring it to life:

EXILE is a glamour word. It has undertones of tragedy. But at Ciampino airport in Rome yesterday there wasn't a vestige of glamour, and tragedy had yet to set in.

A man running away, however compelling his reason, is undignified. A king running away is embarrassing. Embarrassing to the country to which he flees. Embarrassing to the handful of officials who have been hurriedly awakened and sent to the airport, and who have not even had time to bathe and probably still have their pyjamas on under their uniforms.

What do you say? "Welcome, your majesty." Perhaps you do, but as soon as the words are uttered you realise how inappropriate they sound, and you busy yourself with looking after the luggage coming off the aircraft: the seven suitcases, the white puppy and the portable radio. What incredible clutter people pack when they leave in a hurry.

No, you didn't say that to the king, who had now moved off across the tarmac to a bleak future, relieved only by the prospect of a voluminous autobiography serialised in a Sunday paper.

Suddenly the readers have something to think about. They see the picture in a new and different light. An act of creation has taken place. It would have been very different if the caption had merely said:

King Constantine of Greece and his family arriving in Rome yesterday after their hurried flight.

---

*A pure invention, I rush to say.

This is an example of a caption snatched from thin air. Its quiet tone catches the atmosphere of the situation. The caption that follows does the same thing in an entirely different way. It appeared during a rail go-slow under a picture of a union leader standing by a model of a railway engine, and that is all the non-caption sub would have found to say about it. But a *Daily Mail* sub-editor brought out the piquancy of the situation:

FEW men can resist a model train. Enthusiasm is not dampened by having driven a real one. Ask the man in the picture.

He is Mr Albert Griffiths, 59, general secretary of the Associated Society of Locomotive Engineers and Firemen.

The model is at ASLEF's headquarters at Hampstead. The engine is from the steam era when guards travelled in the back of the train and everyone was happy with the arrangement.

Serious students of locomotion will notice that Mr Griffiths had a finger on the brake yesterday . . .

Note the slow build-up, and the piling of fact upon fact, and then the rather pedantic phrase "serious students of locomotion" which leads beautifully to the crunch point.

It frequently happens that a picture is appealing but unnewsy. The sub needs then to find some peg on which to hang the project. A good example, which appeared in the *Daily Mail,* was a snap of a child model pulling up her knickers at a Paris fashion show. Although it had just happened it was a timeless, dateless, magaziny sort of picture. But the *Mail* was currently receiving thousands of letters from readers suggesting "Pillow Thoughts". This one was reproduced from the previous day's paper:

Things that give one confidence: NEW ELASTIC IN ONE'S PANTIES
And the caption below read:

NEW elastic in one's panties may give one confidence. But it seems that particular Pillow Thought never occurred to this little girl.

She had new elastic yesterday. She had new everything, because she was one of the models in a fashion show. But she didn't seem very confident about things staying up on their own.

Elegance was forgotten as she gave her panties a reassuring tug . . .
And, quite naturally, it gives rise to a new Pillow Thought.

Contradictory Things: *Children.*

All the three captions quoted have one thing in common: they have but one basic fact. Everything else is added by the imaginative writer. Instead of dismissing the caption in one sentence he has provided something more to occupy and titillate the reader.

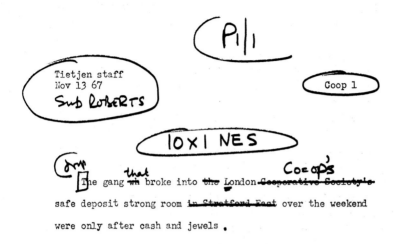

CP|1

Tietjen staff
Nov 13 67
Sub ROBERTS

Coop 1

10 X 1 NES

The gang *that* broke into ~~the~~ London ~~Cooperative Society's~~ Co=ops'
safe deposit strong room ~~in Stratford East~~ over the weekend
were only after cash and jewels .

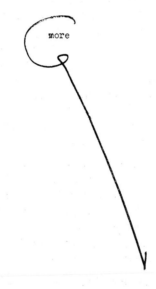

more

Plate 1   Copy that needed few marks, all neat and tidy for
the Printer

8 X 1

They helped themselves to ~~untold~~ thousands of pounds in Treasury notes and articles of jewellery, ~~and discarded gold~~ but left ~~sovereigns,~~ premium bonds and ~~other documents.~~ securities.

~~Once inside the vast safe deposit the gang had no pattern to work to.~~ In a higgledy-piggledy fashion they broke open abt 120 of the 625 deed boxes in the vault in Stratford, E.

~~They went from shelf to shelf leaving many untouched.~~

~~The figure of £1,000,000 has been given as the total loss but this has been described as "unrealistic".~~

It will take months before the full extent of the ~~robbery~~ loss is ~~clear,~~ ~~known~~ as the contents of the boxes ~~in the vault~~ are known only to the owners. And then many of ~~these will not come forward~~ them may be reluctant to reveal their private fortunes.

~~Scotland Yard~~ C. Police know ~~that~~ the thermic lance used ~~by the safebreakers~~ to cut through the ~~two-ft~~ 2ft- thick steel doors ~~and the grill into the strong room~~ was stolen from a West London factory ten days ago.

Indent 24

end indent

more

Plate 2   A lot of subbing marks, but still clear for the
Printer

114

Plates 3 and 4   Both blocks occupying the same area, but the second gains enormously by its boldness. The print could have been cropped in many ways, but in this case the girl's legs were no great loss

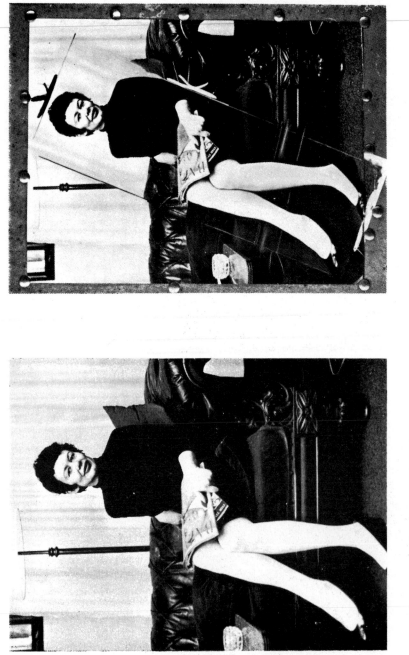

Plate 6   Cut-marks on the tilt, sofa straightened and foot painted in by retoucher

Plate 5   Most of the plate is waste, and unmanageable as a single-column picture

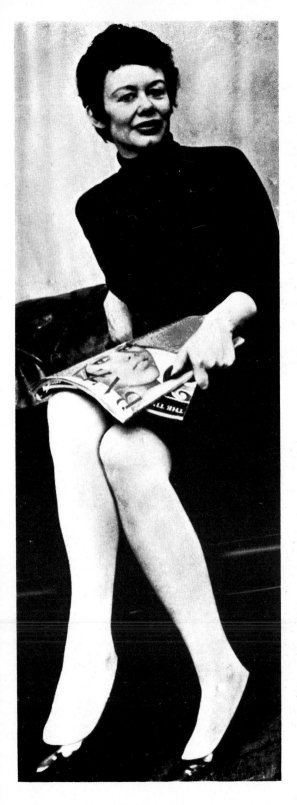

Plate 7 Finished block for original shown in Plate 5. Almost all the waste has been eliminated

117

Plate 8 Attractive as a square block, but there are other permutations, even with such an unlikely subject

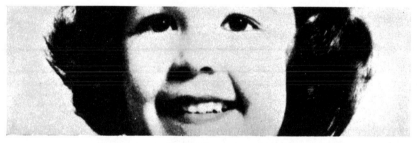

Plate 9 The landscape: It could head a 4-column feature and give a dramatic touch to the page

Plate 10 A gay tilt, changing the atmosphere of the picture

Plate 11 Tilted the opposite way, for a bright come-on look

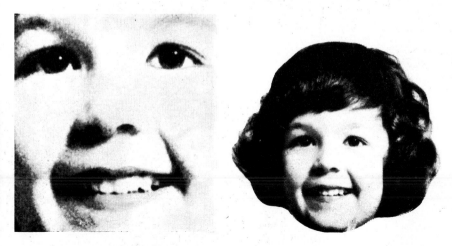

Plate 12 The cut-right-in to bring out the features. The loss of hair is a pity but sometimes this is necessary

Plate 13 The mask or guillotine head. An ideal subject for this treatment

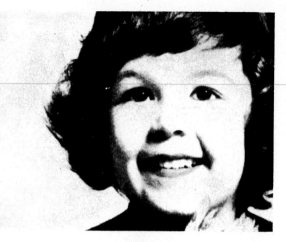

Plate 14 Off-centre and well-cropped in. Leave more tint on the right and it becomes an ideal subject for an overprint

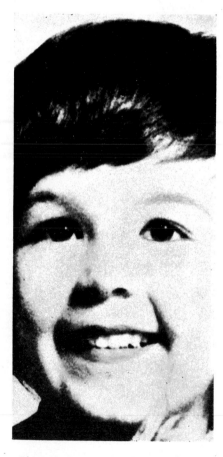

Plate 15 Cut in close each side. The least-successful treatment for this face, but many heads do lend themselves to this kind of cropping

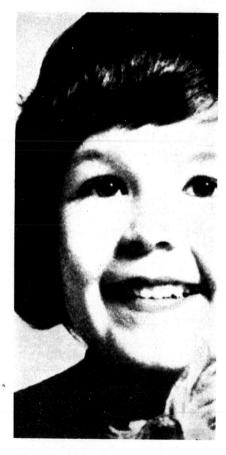

Plate 16 Much better. The off-centre close-cropping gives the picture an off-beat, featurish air

Make that intro sing

But this does not mean the only creative work takes place on what are sometimes known in a derogatory way as "flam" captions. Even when there is a full story and a plethora of facts it is possible to approach the caption in such a way as to capture the reader's imagination from the start. I give three examples of the opening sentences of story captions on newsy pictures.

From *The Mirror*, on a superb picture of a football match in a blizzard:

THE weather we've been having lately might make lesser mortals quake in their snow boots. But we Great Sporting Britons have been through this sort of thing before. And the men who are made on our playing fields face adversity with fortitude.

From the *Sun* on a picture of a small queue outside the Public Records Office:

THE WORLD of scholarship was in no undignified hurry yesterday to lay hands on Government documents released to public view under the new 30-year rule.

From the *Daily Mail*, on an entertaining picture of a Lord Mayor wearing nothing but his chain of office in a sauna bath:

EVEN with his clothes off yesterday James Meadows was not as other men. He was still, quite plainly, the Lord Mayor of Birmingham.

Each of these opening sentences does a great job of scene-setting. They do some of the reader's thinking for him, in the sense that they plant in his mind a thought that he probably wouldn't have had for himself:

The ironic hark-back to the Playing Fields of Eton;

The slightly tongue-in-cheek reference to the dignified world of scholarship;

The intentionally-deflating suggestion that a Lord Mayor is not as other men.

Not all this kind of work falls to the sub, although it does more often than not. When he has got a picture caption ready-made he can leave well alone. Take, for example, this opening sentence composed by a feature writer, on a scene from *The Boy Friend:*

SWINGING London, according to Twiggy, is dead. I think that the thing which will finally bury it is the revival of Sandy Wilson's The Boy Friend, opening at the Comedy Theatre tonight.

Before reading that, would anyone have thought it possible to say anything even slightly original about *The Boy Friend?* No wise sub would attempt to improve on it. He has too many demands on his skill to waste time using it where it's not needed.

What abaht the mechanics?

I have dealt up to now with story captions — the real challenging stuff. But most pictures don't have this kind of thing attached. The bulk of newspaper photographs are those which go with stories — "not so much a picture, more an illustration" as someone sagely put it. These also need handling with due care and attention, and they can do with a bit of ingenuity, too.

There are certain basic things to note, some of them largely mechanical.

RULE 1: ALWAYS CHECK THE CROP MARKS.

Some subs have dropped more clangers than seems humanly possible just by not making this an unbreakable rule. It is vital to see the print before writing the caption: it is no less vital to know *how much* of the print will appear in the block. I have known a sub be given a print showing a group of eight people without being told that four of them have been cropped off, and only by the sheerest chance has disaster been averted.

The newspaper looks daft if the caption says:

Vanessa Redgrave leaves the theatre with her pet dog . . .

and the block or bromide only shows either (a) Vanessa or (b) the dog. It's not much better to have a caption reading:

Lord Snowdon, wearing knee-length boots with a dinner jacket, arrives . . . if some Charlie has cut the boots off to get the right fit.

RULE 2: WATCH YOUR TENSES.

Some subs, and therefore some newspapers, get in a terrible muddle with tenses in the opening sentence of captions. This usually arises out of trying to combine a present-tense verb with "yesterday":

In thigh-high skirt and sky-high hat, starlet Gilda Sparkle arrives at London Airport yesterday . . .

Mrs Gladys Wilson examines a book of romantic verse at an exhibition in London last night . . .

One undesirable way to get out of this is by the use of *Telegraph*ese:

Miss Gilda Sparkle arriving at London Airport yesterday. Miss Sparkle . . .

Mrs Gladys Wilson examining a book of romantic verse last night. Mrs Wilson . . .

This is the way to a dull, lifeless caption — and the cause is the opening non-sentence. The best way out is to separate the verb and the time by making it clear that they are two distinct thoughts, and cutting them off by a colon or leaders or even a full stop, or by dispensing with the verb altogether:

Thigh-high skirt, sky-high hat . . . this was starlet Gilda Sparkle at London Airport yesterday.

Examining a book of romantic verse: Mrs Gladys Wilson at yester-day's . . .

This way the reader doesn't get in a muddle with his time scale.

RULE 3: RELATE IT TO THE STORY.

There is one set of circumstances in which a head-only picture can get by with a name-only caption. This is when the picture is very small and is dropped in a heading, or between a heading and a story. In this case anything more than a couple of words of 6 point bold close up to the block is obtrusive and typographically jarring.

But in all other cases the sub should use the caption to say something worthwhile, and provide a link with the story. On the routine single-column block the old *Time*-style caption has never been bettered. This consists of two distinct lines, usually the top one in bold caps and the other in italic lower case:

JENKINS
A new, tough line

If there is more than one picture it is useful to establish a theme to catch the reader's eye:

STIMPSON
Guilty of murder

ROSS
Guilty of robbery

HOWELL
Innocent of both

Note that no full points are necessary.

Occasionally it is convenient to use the theme in the caps line and the name in the second:

GUILTY
of murder: Stimpson

GUILTY
of robbery: Ross

NOT GUILTY
of either: Howell

The idea of the two separate thoughts inherent in *Time* captions can be usefully employed in one-line captions across broader measure:

Jiving with Miss Flossie Trout: Mr Gordon Walker
In scarlet kimono . . . Mick Jagger at Elmers End
The Archbishop: Strong attack, stout defence

Here, because there is no pretence at a complete sentence, the lack of active verbs does not result in any loss of vigour. The short, sharp phrases have the totally opposite effect of introducing a sense of urgency.

RULE 4: DON'T SAY IT ALL TWICE.

A common failing in some newspapers is to duplicate the story intro in the caption. As these are usually the same papers which have already repeated the intro in the fifth par of the story it can become quite boring.

What is even worse is for the caption to retell practically the entire story in different words, as well as repeating the intro, and often the heading as well.

This is sometimes the fault of the newspaper's style. If the sub is required to write a four-line caption across four columns the likelihood is that he's got more words than he can reasonably use, and will have to pad from the story.

Take this absolutely-genuine, unaltered, front-page example.

First comes a 7-column heading over a 7-column picture:

WHEELS OF WONDER AS TWO MILLION
FLOCK TO FESTIVAL OF FAITH

I'm not sure what that means, but the picture shows the top of a lot of buses, and the caption underneath (three lines across 7 columns) reads:

An aerial view of the buses, trucks and other forms of transport which carried two million Zion Christian Church followers to their annual Easter conference at Moria City, near Pietersburg. More than 100 church choirs sang at the three-day ceremony, which saw devotees of Southern Africa's fastest-growing church queue for hours to place cash contributions in heavily-guarded strongboxes. The church is headed by Bishop Barnabas Lekganyane, 29, who yesterday expressed his gratitude for the fantastic turn-out.

Now you might think that is the whole story, but you'd be wrong. Underneath is a single-column heading that says:

MILLIONS
FLOCK TO
Z C C
MEETING

You'll notice that in the headings alone we have the MILLIONS and the FLOCK TO twice, which suggests that the left hand knoweth not what the right hand doeth. But wait . . . here's the story:

BISHOP Barnabas Lekganyane, head of the Zionist Christian Church, yesterday expressed his gratitude for the support of about 2-million worshippers who converged on Moria, near Pietersburg, for the church's Easter conference.

The 29-year-old bishop, also known as Ramarumo, attended the mass open-air conference of the ZCC, Southern Africa's fastest-growing church, in a green suit with a yellow insert at the side.

He led drum majorettes to a green-carpeted altar where they knelt and greeted worshippers with the word "Kgotsong!" (Let there be peace).

A deafening response of "A e ate!" (Let it spread), was followed by a lengthy hand-clapping and handkerchief waving by loyal church members.

More than 100 church choirs from all over South Africa sang throughout the three-day gathering.

By 4.30 pm yesterday, as is tradition in the ZCC, 15 000 people had already been baptised in a river adjoining the church.

The worshippers will trek back home again today.

A quick glance will show that the readers already know from the caption they couldn't miss reading for starters:

- Everything in the first par
- Almost everything in the second
- Everything in the fifth.

All that the caption needed to say was *DROPPING IN FOR A HYMN AND A PRAYER . . . Heaven's eye view of just some of the buses that carried the faithful yesterday.*

You could set that to music and play it on your harp.

RULE 5: WATCH THOSE SERIES CAPTIONS.

The points made in Rule 4 apply with equal vigour if you've got a series of pictures relating to a story.

It's bad enough to have the intro repeated in one caption but to have it repeated in three borders on absurdity. In a series in front of me . . .

CAPTION A quite properly identifies the couple in the picture (albeit with too much detail) then gives a summary of the accompanying story:

It was the telephone call of a lifetime yesterday for Mr Cedric de Villiers and his fiancée, Miss Monika Kuerton, when they surprised both sets of parents — at the same time — by announcing they were getting married. The phone call linked Germany, Rustenburg, and Johannesburg.

CAPTION B identifies the people, and then repeats details already given in the story and in caption A:

It was all smiles yesterday for Mr Hugo de Villiers and his wife Eunice of Rustenburg who were surprised to learn of their son's intended marriage via a special phone call.

CAPTION C does likewise, and then repeats the details already given in the story and in Caption A and in Caption B:

Mr Erich Jakob and his wife Hildegard of Dusseldorf in West Germany who were linked up to Rustenburg and Johannesburg to hear the thrilling news of their daughter's engagement.

This could obviously go on indefinitely by adding more relations or even drawing in passers-by from the street, until all the readers knew it by heart and could use it as a soporific instead of counting sheep.

And all that's really needed is:

● *JO'BURG CALLING . . . Cedric and Monika give the news simultaneously to boths mums and dads in Rustenburg and Dusseldorf.*

● *RUSTENBURG HERE . . . a surprise for Cedric's parents.*

● *DUSSELDORF HERE . . . a thrill for Monika's parents.*

RULE 6: KEEP A CAPTION UNDERNEATH.

Do that even if it's only a 6-point line, and even if there's a fully detailed story caption running alongside the block.

There are few things more calculated to irritate the reader than to force him to read several paragraphs of copy before reaching the magic words "Rosie (left)".

However many explanatory words there may be elsewhere on the page, each picture needs an instant-recognition aid *underneath.* As a reader I find myself bemused by the practice followed by some magazines of using one caption to cover several pictures, even to the point that it's difficult to tell which picture is being referred to:

The 217th Spitfire (left) to go into action from Biggin Hill (bottom left) was flown by Flying Officer Heroe (extreme left, third from left), who collapsed while receiving the DFC (bottom right) from the King (below), recovered sufficiently to take part in the VE-Day parade (arrowed, top right) but died soon afterwards and was buried in the country churchyard at Blowing Top (see cover).

Always remember that the caption is there to make it easy for the reader, not to test his intelligence.

RULE 7: DON'T OVERDO IT.

The caption gives the sub his greatest opportunity for creative writing, and therein lies a danger.

IT'S EASY to hype a caption so much that it looks naive to the point of being ludicrous.

Take this on a picture of a moderately pretty girl holding a ball and standing behind a set of stumps:

Natal and Eastern Province cricketers do not look like JULIE LEWELL, yet thousands of spectators are still expected to flock to the Wanderers in Johannesburg on Friday evening when these two teams meet in the final of the Benson and Hedges series.

Well, of course they don't look like Julie because to start with they're chaps. And spectators flock to the Wanderers to watch cricket, not girls.

I suppose it could have worked in the hands of a caption-writing genius on the *Sun* or *The Mirror*, but done with a heavy hand like this 'tis better not tried at all.

IT'S EASY, also, to fall into the trap of being atrociously twee, or of over-writing, or being sentimental to the point of soppiness, and it happens by trying too hard. I have quoted elsewhere the words of a former editor of the *Daily Mail* on the subject, and I propose to quote them again, because they should be engraved on every caption-writer's heart:

Let us resolve never to have another picture caption which purports to tell us what a child of eight months or an Aberdeen terrier would say if either of them could speak. Let us stop, once and for all, those whimsical, folksy captions which may have been fashionable thirty years ago, but which today must make our readers sick over the side . . .

So — try a real writing job, but do it with caution.

One final note: It will be noticed that a number of the rules suggested for subbing news stories have been broken in the captions above. That is as it should be. Writing an accompaniment for a picture is an entirely different art, in which the picture is the intro, the attention-catcher, and the rest can fall more gently into place.

Sizing Jane Fonda up for a block

THE first sentence of the first paragraph on the first page of my first Latin primer consisted of these three words:

DISCIPULI PICTURAM SPECTATE

which, being freely translated means:

LOOK AT THAT PICTURE TILL YOUR EYES ACHE

And this is really the first lesson in picture-cropping. Study the picture, and consider which is the best way it can be cut to exclude all that is unnecessary, and shine a spotlight on all that is virtuous in it. The popular national newspapers crop pictures to their best advantage. Some provincial papers do. But many provincial and weekly newspapers do not even begin to understand what there is to be gained by sharp and even brutal cutting.

It is true that there are occasions when the immediate reaction to a picture is: *We must give the whole frame, or something will be lost.* But this is a rare happening, the once-in-a-thousand chance. The other 999 pictures gain by having something cut out. This is particularly important when the relation between the size of the original and the size of the block is borne in mind. A sharply-defined 15-inch by 12-inch glossy print of the Critchley Hunt setting out from the Bull Inn at Hollingworth may look fine in *Country Life*. But brought down to $7\frac{1}{2}$ inches by 6 inches — an area reduction of 75 per cent — and broken up by a 65 screen, the effect is quite hopeless.

This question of size and area reduction should be constantly borne in mind when sizing up pictures for blocks — or screened bromides as they often are these days.* If you have a print 12 inches wide showing the chairman of the Beelzebub Women's Institute presenting the membership shield to Miss Eliza Thrush the background-head-background-head-background proportions will probably be something like this:

$2\frac{1}{2}$in — 2in — 3in — 2in — $2\frac{1}{2}$in

If from this print a 3 inch wide block is made the heads will be only half

---

*For simplicity, in the rest of this chapter please read "block" as covering both.

an inch across, and after maltreatment at the hands of a jobbing process firm and a clapped-out rotary press, Miss Thrush will probably be indistinguishable from the chairman of Beelzebub Rotary Club.

Drastic cropping can improve this situation. Cut through the backs of the heads of the two people and 3 inches is saved on either side, and when the block is made the width reduction is halved. Instead of having a whole head half an inch across you will have three-quarters of a head (and the important three-quarters) one inch across.

The effect of highlighting one part of a picture by cutting in is illustrated in its simplest form in Plates 3 and 4. But this is not the end of it. Cut-marks can be used to bring out the best features of a girl, for example. If she has long elegant legs the cuts should be very close to her legs and parallel to them. If she's a big bosomy bird with thick ankles the ankles should be left out of it and the big bosomy bit highlighted. If she's got a winning, winsome smile but the rest of her looks as though it were not born but laid down on Clydeside, then it's best to concentrate on cropping her face to the best advantage.

This does not necessarily mean straight cuts. Never overlook the possibility of "tilting" or making the cuts at an angle. This is often necessary when sizing up the girl with the lovely long legs mentioned above. There are still an extraordinary number of cameramen around who cannot visualise their pictures in the newspaper, and take snaps of girls half-sideways with their legs out of line with the rest of their body. This is all very well if the subject is a model, sitting against an elegant background, who is going to end up as a 3 column by 10 inch block. But if it's Maisie Flack, photographed with a background of repulsive wallpaper and lucky to make a 5 inch-deep single column, the picture is useless as it stands.

If her legs are left in, her head will be half an inch across and three-quarters of the picture will be wallpaper. If one leg is cut off in the cause of compactness she'll look deformed. The answer is usually to cut the block on the slant, if necessary blowing back the background so that the furniture doesn't appear to be taking off.

Plates 5, 6 and 7 make this point with a picture of Janey Ironside. Note how the cut-marks indicated have made it possible to use the picture boldly in quite a small space.

One final point about cutting on the slant: don't trust to your eyes to get the angles right. Keep a set square handy.

Get the best out of it

So much for waste and highlights. These are really the mechanics of the matter, the things that every sub concerned with pictures should know.

Where the mechanics end the artistry begins, and here there is one thought that should always be present:

THERE ARE MANY, MANY DIFFERENT WAYS OF CROPPING ANY ONE PICTURE

What are the motives for seeking out these different ways? There are two, and they inevitably overlap:

1. TO BRING OUT the best in a picture in relation to its context — if it's a glamorous story to crop the print so that it looks as glamorous as possible; and the same if it's sad, or glad, or brutal, or moody.

Most pictures can be influenced in one direction or another by intelligent cut marks. Some are more easy to influence than others, but none is impossible. For Plates 8 to 16 I have deliberately chosen the most difficult of all — a round-faced child photographed full face — and shown nine ways of dealing with it. The original print, in fact, had a body attached, and had that been brought into use the nine permutations could easily have become ninety.

Note how each of the blocks has a subtle difference of atmosphere at first glance — and that is all that most face pictures get. It is particularly marked in the two cut on the slant.

2. TO BRING OUT the best in a picture in relation to the page. The most useful weapon in creating a dramatic page is a dramatic picture. That is blindingly obvious. *But the picture need not be inherently dramatic.* It may be a perfectly ordinary picture — dramatically cut.

The man who visualises every page drawn round a picture 3 columns by 6 inches will end up with a lot of dull pages. What he should be doing is looking for ways of avoiding pictures measuring 3 columns by 6 inches. For this is a fundamental truth about the use of pictures in newspapers:

THE IMPACT OF A BLOCK GROWS THE FURTHER IT DEPARTS FROM SQUARE

The very deep block catches the eye. The very wide block does likewise. And the moral is to aim all the time at a strong vertical or horizontal stress.

Never become tied to the view that a picture is naturally 2 columns by 4 inches or 3 columns by 5 inches. If it's all that natural it will make no impact at all. The job of the chap sizing up the picture is actively to search for the virtues and highlights and stresses which will convert it from a mundane squarish block into a dramatic 2 columns by 14 inches or 6 columns by 3 inches — and both *are* sometimes possible with the same picture.

This fluidity of approach can revolutionise the design of a page, and turn the mundane into the eye-catching.

Sometimes the eccentric works

Up to this point I have dealt only with the straightforward treatment of pictures. The straightforward is usually the best. Why sully a perfectly good block by piling it high with gimmicks? The effect is often to lose the impact it had in the first place. But there are some circumstances in which a less orthodox approach is called for.

1. *When there is an area of waste in a picture that can't be eliminated by careful cropping or tilting.*

PIERCES can be used to contain the headline or caption. But never let the piercing treatment get out of hand. It is a good rule never to pierce *except* on a waste area of block, and then to do it boldly.

If a pierce needs forcing it's a bad one, and is probably cutting out something that ought to be in. Be careful, also, that a pierce does not interfere with the visual merit of the picture: if, for example, the picture shows a mum gazing adoringly at a baby in a pram the pierce should not cut the line between mum's eyes and the baby, because this will lessen the effect.

Pierces need not always be rectangular, even when the printing method is letterpress. There is no serious problem in cutting out circular or oval pierces on the block itself. Cutting odd-shaped holes in the base is a different matter, so the heading or text to be dropped in should be based on a rectangle or square which will fit in the hole.

If an odd-shaped headline is wanted in a pierce it is easy with the offset process. With letterpress the only satisfactory methods are to have the block made as a line-and-tone combine, or to make the heading as a separate line job and have it stuck in the hole in the half-tone.

THREE-SIDED CUT-OUTS can be useful not only to eliminate waste but also to link a picture with a story by running in a headline:

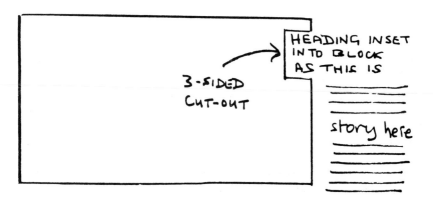

With this kind of operation it is even more important to resist the temptation to cut as a gimmick instead of to eliminate waste. Sometimes the most extraordinary contortions are produced. I've never actually seen anyone decapitated in the cause of a three-sided cut, but I did once see a delicious actress with her head attached to her body by the merest thread.

The cut-out should not be more than an eighth of an inch from the top of the block unless the space alongside the top bit is to be used for straplines, otherwise the surplus white space will throw the heading off balance.

OVERPRINTS are a good device to utilise waste, but have the disadvantages that with letterpress the blocks take much longer to make. They also tend to give news pages a featurish appearance.

Overprints can be either black on a light-background print or white on a dark background (but beware — the second process is even slower because it involves a line-and-tone combine). It either case it is usually desirable to have the background which takes the lettering blown back to a fairly even tint to make sure that the words come over loud and clear.

2. *When an odd shape will contribute to making a dramatic block, or (and this is more usual) a dramatic page.*

THE MASK, or guillotine head as it's still sometimes known, is the most common deviation from the straightforward rectangle. This is now less popular than it used to be, perhaps because like so many other good things it was overdone and unsuitable subjects were chosen. Ideally it must be possible to cut cleanly and completely round the head. For this reason a girl with shoulder-length hair can't be masked, and a chap with a jutting-out pipe makes a bad mask because the block is thrown off balance. Profiles are also difficult because it's practically impossible to find a cut-mask for the neck which doesn't look as though it's been attended to by a guillotine.*

The short hair and round head of the child in Plate 13, combined with the fact that the photograph is absolutely full face, make her an ideal subject for masking.

THE CIRCULAR or oval block is not subject to so many difficulties as the mask, because bits of the face or hair can be cut off at any point. But this is a treatment that should be kept for the rarest occasion. It is the purest gimmick, in that it is totally unfunctional. Used once in a blue moon, small in a puff or big in a fashion page, it has its effect by its extraordinariness. But that is all there is to it.

---

*A glance at a coin with a king's head on it will show what I mean. On the current Elizabeth II coins the designers have attached a bit of body.

THE SLANTED block has its uses, but because of its featurish effect and the setting difficulties it creates it should be used with caution on news pages. The point made about pierces applies with even greater force: never cut a block on the slant unless it actually improves it. Most slanted blocks are simple parallelograms leaning either backwards or forwards, and they are only really effective, and really justified, when they embrace a figure leaning backwards or forwards. If it's a picture of Shirley Bassey doing her night club bit, holding out her arms to clutch the men in the audience, that's a natural forward slope. If she's doing her characteristic arms-back-stomach-forward bit that's a natural backward slope. But if she's standing up straight that's a simple rectangle and that's all there is to *that*.

MULTI-SIDED blocks — five-, six-, seven-, or nineteen-sided, should also be kept for very rare use, and then only used small. The ideal situation is the gimmicky Page One puff drawing attention either to goodies inside or goodies to come next week.

3. *When the use of some kind of border will improve the appearance of the block or the page.*

The trend today is to simple plain-edged blocks. In the *Daily Mail* in Lord Northcliffe's day the photographic reproductions were a sight for artistic eyes. The very fact of their presence was emphasised not merely by the borders that surrounded them, but by decorative scrolls and flourishes, laboriously drawn in by artists who should have been devoting their attention to higher things. The idea of borders persisted, and indeed the majority of local papers still shy away from the plain edge, and use very fine borders, sometimes made even worse by a white scratch-line inside.

The real lesson of this is that the plain edge is best. But, nevertheless, a border can sometimes be used to bring out the best in a picture.

The Mirror is a good paper to watch for the effective use of heavy black borders. Some newspapermen, particularly those working on journals selling fewer than 5,000 copies a week, are prone to make sneering remarks like: "When's the funeral?" Yet for some purposes the thick black border, particularly when combined with rounded corners (see below), is a most efficient attracter of attention.

An ideal subject is the elegant fashion picture, particularly one in which the background is strictly waste but in fact adds an indefinable atmosphere. A seven-foot tall black model wearing clothes by a trendy designer and standing with arms and legs outstretched against a white sheet would provide the perfect occasion for the black border.

Tint borders have a lot to contribute, especially in the fashion field. But never forget that, like so many other things mentioned in this chapter, they tend to detract from the newsiness of a page.

Both tint and black borders are useful for extending a print to provide an artificial pierce for text or headlines:

Note the rounded corners inside the tint border — an essentially featurish device. This kind of block is at its best when it occupies the whole of the top of a page.

Given a reasonable retouch artist it is not, of course, necessary to use a border when extending a print to create a pierce. The natural tones of the picture itself can be extended to continue round the pierce, but they need blending with great care or the join will show.

4. *When some special effect is needed, usually to give a page a particular character.*

ROUNDED CORNERS are a handy device for this purpose, but need to be used with caution. If every other picture in the paper has rounded corners any useful purpose is lost. They should be kept for the occasional formal, set-piece picture, or the series of matching blocks running across a page. In this way they are made to work for their living.

DOT PRINTS come into their own in providing motifs for series or continuing stories. I have found the most satisfactory method is to reduce a 15 inch by 12 inch print to a 1½ inch wide block, and then make a 15 by 12 print from the process negative.

LINEN SCREENS can be used to give a dignified, Old Masterish finish to suitable pictures. Again this is a treatment to be used only occasionally, because in some way it lessens the newsy vigour of a picture.

LINE PRINTS from halftones can be used in much the same way as dot prints. Note, however, that they should be used only with faces or objects that are readily recognisable because of the amount of definition they lose.

A touch of the Hammersmiths

This last section is devoted to the art of repairing the unrepairable: to making a good picture out of a mediocre one, or making one good picture out of two or three mediocre ones. Often, when all else has failed, the situation has been saved by two simple things readily available in all offices:

A PAIR OF SCISSORS AND A STEADY HAND

They are used to cut the waste out of the *middle* of a picture, which is then joined up and retouched so that nobody would ever know. In more complicated cases they are used to cut the best out of two pictures, which are then united in unholy matrimony.

I think it was the distinguished Mr Arthur Brittenden who first used the phrase A Hammersmith Job to describe the technique, thereby honouring the surgeons at that distinguished hospital who were actually doing it with human flesh.

A Hammersmith Job can be as simple as this:

But it can also involve several prints, with a face from one picture, a body from a second, and a grandfather clock from a third.

Modern science has no limits when it comes to Hammersmiths. But as the Old Thunderer once said: there *is* a moral issue. This kind of operation should never be carried out if there could be the slightest moral objection.

Oh, Mr Univers, are you the type for me ?

ALL subs need a certain minimum knowledge of typography, but the minimum is pretty low. The sub whose greatest ambition is to stay in the long grass and keep his head down can get by with a few basic essentials. But the sub who wants to move into executive jobs, at any rate on popular newspapers, needs not only a thorough knowledge of type but also the kind of feel for it which will enable him to design successful pages.

A knowledge of and an aptitude for typography and design are now an essential part of the equipment of an executive on the production side of most newspapers. This is as it should be. I have plugged constantly the point that the only really successful newspaper pages come from the newspaperman-typographer.

The reason for this is simple. A newspaper is about news, and not about design. It exists to sell news, and not design. The pure designer can neither grasp nor learn to live with this fundamental fact. HE is concerned only with getting the best design, but this is only half of it. THE NEWSPAPER is concerned with getting the best design *within the context of what is happening at any given moment.*

For a newspaper the news and the design are an absolutely inseparable part of the same process. It is possible to put into a page the most exciting and stimulating news stories, and yet have it not only unappetising but also unreadable. It is also possible to create a page which sends the artists among us into paroxysms of delight, yet is not exciting or stimulating from a newspaper point of view. A page may be well-balanced and beautiful and elegant, but still a disaster because it bears no relation to the news.

The only man who is in a position to create a dynamic newspaper page is the newspaperman who knows about type.

A sub who has some expertise in this field has an advantage over his colleagues on the table who don't. He is the one who will be called upon to draw a page, and he will have taken the first step in the direction of the editor's chair.

But first: what are the kind of things a sub ought to know about type? I have set out below some of the most basic things.

How type is measured

The size of type is measured in points, a point being 0.01383 inch, which give approximately 72 points to the inch.

This measurement refers not to the size of any given letter, but to the depth of the body on which the letter stands. In hot metal, the actual face size is always less than the body size because of the bevels top and bottom.

In rough and ready terms (but near enough to be a handy subs' guide) the points size approximates to the total size of the lower case alphabet, from the top of the highest ascender to the bottom of the lowest descender.

It follows from this that a 72 point capital letter of any upper and lower case fount is considerably smaller in appearing size than 72 points, because the size of the letter has to allow for the descenders in the lower case alphabet dropping below its own level. The example in 72 pt Bodoni Bold demonstrates the point:

The descenders on the p and the q are, it can be seen, an integral part of the type size. There is an obvious exception to this: the all-capital display founts known as titling caps. These founts, which include the much-used Lining Gothic and Times Titling, frequently occupy all or nearly all the depth of the body.

One factor to be considered in relation to the size of type is that although two faces may be of the same size one of them may *look* very much bigger. This is caused to a large extent by the variations in what is known as the *x*-height of different types.

The *x*-height is simply the height of the letter *x*, or of any other lower case letter without an ascender or descender. If the *x*-height is big in proportion to the size of type it is known as "big on the body" and the ascenders and descenders will be proportionately smaller. The converse also applies.

The extent of the variation is shown in this line of letters:

aaaaaa

All are 30 point letters, from left to right Bodoni Bold, Schoolbook Bold, Caslon, Grotesque Bold Extended, Gill Sans Bold and Placard Bold Condensed.

The effect of the variation in *x*-height can be seen when two words are set side by side, one Bodoni Bold, the other Schoolbook Bold, *both* 30 point:

Rough Rough

Note the differing sizes of the ascenders and descenders. The difference is equally marked between Grotesque Condensed and Placard Condensed, which is much bigger on the body:

Roughneck Roughneck

The optical effect of a type face is also influenced by what is loosely called its *colour*, which itself consists of two factors, *weight* and *width*.

The heavier and wider a face is, the more emphatic its appearance. The first, weight, can be demonstrated by this example of 24 point Bodoni, Bodoni Bold, and Bodoni Ultra Bold:

top top **top**

The effect of the second, width, can be seen when 30 point Grotesque Bold Condensed is set alongside 30 point Grotesque Bold Extended:

chicken chicken

The most dramatic contrast is between a light, narrow face with a small *x*-height and a heavy, wide face with a large *x*-height:

Both are 36 point, the first in the elegant, rather-bookish Bembo, the second in the thumping, rather-clumsy Gill Sans Ultra Bold.

The usual range of setting for text sizes in British newspapers is 4¾, 5, 6, 7, 8, 9, 10, 12 and 14 point, with occasionally 18 point. Display sizes are normally 14, 18, 24, 30, 36, 42, 48, 60, 72 point and occasionally 84 and 96 point.

The *width* to which type is set is expressed not in points but in 12 point or pica ems. The em is the square of any given body depth, so a 12 point or pica em is 12 points (one pica) wide. Column widths are always measured in pica ems — known as picas in America and computer talk (the em being understood) and ems in most English newspapers (the pica being understood). This often leads to confusion when em is used in its precise literal sense.

An example of this is when a story is sent to the Printer (hot metal variety) marked "em each side". This is taken not as a pica em but as an em of the body — 6 points in a story set in 6 point, 8 points in an 8 point story and so on.

Printers often get over this confusion by using the word *mutton* for an em in this sense. The word is little used in editorial departments, but the equivalent word for an en (half an em), which is *nut* , is of course in regular use.

Text types and setting variants

A glance at an old newspaper is sufficient to convince any sub of the great advance made in text types during the present century. Most of the new faces are infinitely superior to the old, but I don't propose to go into them here, because the sub has got to be satisfied with what he's got and make the best of it.

What can be usefully dealt with are the questions of settings, indentions, the use of bold and italic, paragraphing, leading, and the many devices that can be employed to bring an otherwise grey mass of text to life.

SETTING STYLES. Apart from standard, full-out, flush-on-column-rule setting, which many newspapers have now abandoned in the cause of lightness and whiteness, there are five setting styles in common use.

It will be noticed that the first three and the last only apply to hot metal setting, because computerised photosetting will adjust the column width at the touch of a key, making indention unnecessary. The five are:

a. Nut each side. Here the whole story is indented an en "of the body" (that is, 4 points in an 8 point story) each side. The setting instructions vary from office to office, and include NES, nuts, nut e/s, ½ e/s and nut each end.

b. Em each side. Again, an em "of the body", written em e/s or 1 e/s.

c. Pica each side. A pica em indent, written pica e/s.

d. Full and one. Here the normal paragraph indention is reversed, so that the first line of a paragraph is set full measure and the rest indented one em left. The setting instructions are full + 1, 0 + 1, reverse indent or hanging indent, according to office practice.

e. Full and one nut right. The same style as *d*, but with a nut indent on the right. Most newspapers prefer this style to *d* because it looks more balanced between the column rules. Setting instructions are the same as for *d* , with nut right or NR added.

This is the effect of the various styles:

Full

Twelve-year-old Gillian Sellers, a pupil at Bromley High School for Girls, was hugged by a yeti at the Boys and Girls Exhibition in London yesterday.

She said later: "It felt just like my sister's teddy bear, but actually I knew there was a man inside."

Nut e/s

Twelve-year-old Gillian Sellers, a pupil at Bromley High School for Girls, was hugged by a yeti at the Boys and Girls Exhibition in London yesterday.

She said later: "It felt just like my sister's teddy bear, but actually I knew there was a man inside."

Em e/s

Twelve-year-old Gillian Sellers, a pupil at Bromley High School for Girls, was hugged by a yeti at the Boys and Girls Exhibition in London yesterday.

She said later: "It felt just like my sister's teddy bear, but actually I knew there was a man inside."

Pica e/s

Twelve-year-old Gillian Sellers, a pupil at Bromley High School for Girls, was hugged by a yeti at the Boys and Girls Exhibition in London yesterday.

She said later: "It felt just like my sister's teddy bear, but actually I knew there was a man inside."

0 + 1

Twelve-year-old Gillian Sellers, a pupil at Bromley High School for Girls, was hugged by a yeti at the Boys and Girls Exhibition in London yesterday.

She said later: "It felt just like my sister's teddy bear, but actually I knew there was a man inside."

0 + 1 NR

Twelve-year-old Gillian Sellers, a pupil at Bromley High School for Girls, was hugged by a yeti at the Boys and Girls Exhibition in London yesterday.

She said later: "It felt just like my sister's teddy bear, but actually I knew there was a man inside."

Warning note: Beware of starting 0 + 1 paragraphs with quote marks. They give a patchy appearance to indention. If the story is full of quotes that's the chief sub's fault and there's nothing the man actually doing the work can do about it.

One other setting variant may be noted for occasional use — that known as unjustified, or sometimes as set left and ragged right. It is at its best in short, well-displayed caption stories or puffs, with liberal leading between pars. The following examples are set in 12 point Helvetica, one with par indents, the other without — a form that I think gives a better balance:

Sitting side by side: Gillian and Philippa Sellers, winners of the children's fancy dress contest in the Reina del Mar somewhere in the Med.

The sisters, aged 12 and six, appeared as Cleopatra and her handmaiden. Both are pupils of Bromley High School for Girls in Kent.

Philippa won her first fancy dress contest when she was two years old. She went as "A Little Bit of Fluff", wearing only a carefully-placed piece of cotton wool.

Sitting side by side: Gillian and Philippa Sellers, winners of the children's fancy dress contest in the Reina del Mar somewhere in the Med.

The sisters, aged 12 and six, appeared as Cleopatra and her handmaiden. Both are pupils of Bromley High School for Girls in Kent.

Philippa won her first fancy dress contest when she was two years old. She went as "A Little Bit of Fluff", wearing only a carefully-placed piece of cotton wool.

INDENTIONS IN TEXT. Let me start by deploring the practice of using 0 + 1 indentions in full out or NES stories. They look more like setting errors than indents. In my view there are only two satisfactory forms of indention:

a. 2 + 1. Here the whole paragraph is indented an additional em left, so that the first line is indented two ems and the rest of the paragraph one; hence the instruction 2 + 1.

b. The whole paragraph indented an em "of the body" each side. This is the comparative effect:

Gillian Sellers, 12-year-old school-girl from Bromley, Kent, took a strong lead in the putting green championships at Minnis Bay yesterday.

The crowd cheered as she five times holed in one — her best achievement so far. She was later congratulated by her opponents.

Gillian, a pupil at Bromley High School for Girls, is staying at a friend's cottage in Birchington.

Gillian Sellers, 12-year-old school-girl from Bromley, Kent, took a strong lead in the putting green championships at Minnis Bay yesterday.

The crowd cheered as she five times holed in one—her best achievement so far. She was later congratulated by her opponents.

Gillian, a pupil at Bromley High School for Girls, is staying at a friend's cottage in Birchington.

141

BLACK AND ITALIC. These text variants are useful but need to be used with discretion. Too much black gives a page a spotty appearance. Too much italic is weakening and greying with many faces, though there are notable exceptions.

The generic term black is used to cover two distinct types of letter — the sans-serif doric

like this and this and this

and the seriffed bold, which is rapidly overtaking it in popularity

like this and this and this

The bold is much more suitable for indented paragraphs than the doric, which tends to stick out like a sore thumb because of its much sharper contrast. For the same reason the bold is better for long story captions.

Here I must repeat my earlier warning about using black and italic in the same paragraph in hot metal or with certain photosetters. The roman on the Linotype or Intertype will be duplexed with *either* the black or the italic, so both in the same paragraph will involve two machines and cutting in.

There are, of course, many keyboard-set sans faces which are suitable for captions and special treatments. Vogue and Metro in their many permutations are in use in large numbers of newspapers, sometimes in unhappy juxtaposition. Among the newer faces gaining ground are Galaxy and the superb Helvetica, which is used for the unjustified setting on page 141. Both have their bold equivalents.

The more sophisticated computerised photosetters will give italic, bold and any number of different type families in one sentence, should any sub be mad enough to ask.

PARAGRAPHING. Good paragraphing is a considerable aid to legibility. For popular newspapers using a narrow column measure the short paragraph, say four to six lines, is easiest for the readers. The optical break of the par indent (and perhaps the thin lead between the pars) gives him a momentary rest before he carries on reading the next thought.

It should be borne in mind, however, that the wider the measure the longer the paragraphs needed. This applies not only to the increasingly-rare newspapers which have seven column — 13¼ em pages, but to more normal newspapers having a rush of wide measure to the head.

A splash set all across 1½ or two columns will have strips of white running across it if the pars are very short, because of the turn lines of two or three words. This will be even more marked if the text has been sized up to 10 or 12 point; the stripes will be 10 and 12 point, too.

A good rule, whatever the measure: Watch for those jacklines or widows or whatever those odd words occupying a whole line are called in your office. They are space-wasting, and too many of them give a patchy appearance to a piece of setting. Cut them out as soon as you see them in proof.

This is particularly important with multi-column captions. A full five-column line turning one or two words is both ugly and hard to read.

LEADING. The correct use of horizontal white space is important to the appearance of a page. It is true that some modern text faces take no harm from being set, say, 7 on 8 point. But excessive leading between the lines in the context of a narrow-column newspaper causes the type to diffuse and weaken. Compare these examples, and note how much *less* readable the very-heavily leaded examples are.

A good reference book on newspaper practice is undoubtedly *Doing it in style*, published by Pergamon. It has been described by Mr Alec Newman, Deputy Director of the National Council for the Training of Journalists, as "the practical newspaperman's Fowler".

8 pt solid

A good reference book on newspaper practice is undoubtedly *Doing it in style*, published by Pergamon. It has been described by Mr Alec Newman, Deputy Director of the National Council for the Training of Journalists, as "the practical newspaperman's Fowler".

8 pt, 2 pt leaded

A good reference book on newspaper practice is undoubtedly *Doing it in style*, published by Pergamon. It has been described by Mr Alec Newman, Deputy Director of the National Council for the Training of Journalists, as "the practical newspaperman's Fowler".

8 pt, 4 pt leaded

A good reference book on newspaper practice is undoubtedly *Doing it in style*, published by Pergamon. It has been described by Mr Alec Newman, Deputy Director of the National Council for the Training of Journalists, as "the practical newspaperman's Fowler".

8 pt, 1 pt leaded

A good reference book on newspaper practice is undoubtedly *Doing it in style*, published by Pergamon. It has been described by Mr Alec Newman, Deputy Director of the National Council for the Training of Journalists, as "the practical newspaperman's Fowler".

8 pt, 3 pt leaded

A good reference book on newspaper practice is undoubtedly *Doing it in style*, published by Pergamon. It has been described by Mr Alec Newman, Deputy Director of the National Council for the Training of Journalists, as "the practical newspaperman's Fowler".

8 pt, 6 pt leaded

143

Therein lies a warning against allowing comps to fling in handfuls of lead regardless.

The place where lead can be used effectively is *between* paragraphs, and indeed there should be some there. For a single column story a 1½ point or a 2 point lead is enough to do the job, but it will take more if necessary for spacing reasons. This shows the effect of various sizes of lead between paragraphs:

A good book on newspaper practice is undoubtedly *Doing it in style*, published by Pergamon Press.

Mr Alec Newman, Deputy Director of the National Council for the Training of Journalists, has described it as "the practical newspaperman's Fowler".

Nothing between pars

A good book on newspaper practice is undoubtedly *Doing it in style*, published by Pergamon Press.

Mr Alec Newman, Deputy Director of the National Council for the Training of Journalists, has described it as "the practical newspaperman's Fowler"

1½ pt between pars

A good book on newspaper practice is undoubtedly *Doing it in style*, published by Pergamon Press.

Mr Alec Newman, Deputy Director of the National Council for the Training of Journalists, has described it as "the practical newspaperman's Fowler".

2 pt between pars

A good book on newspaper practice is undoubtedly *Doing it in style*, published by Pergamon Press.

Mr Alec Newman, Deputy Director of the National Council for the Training of Journalists, has described it as "the practical newspaperman's Fowler".

3 pt between pars

OTHER DEVICES. There are many typographical tricks which can be employed to force grey out and force brightness in. All have their place, but one important rule should always be borne in mind: *don't over-employ them*. I remember a period on the *Daily Express* when the gimmickry was in danger of obscuring the news, and the Great and Good Christiansen suddenly exhorted his staff in one of his celebrated bulletins: "A reader of the *Daily Express* says: 'Don't you think your articles are interesting enough without having to draw particular attention to them by using spots and stars? In today's edition alone I counted 16 spots and 40 stars.' Dear, dear. Are we really dazzling our readers to that extent? CUT DOWN ON SPOTS AND STARS."

This is sound advice. Never forget the tricks, but don't remember them too often. Those that follow are worthy of place at the back of every sub's mind. They are the black caps and the contrasting type to pick out points;

the drop figures, the white on black figures, and the blobs to establish a sequence; and the vertical rule which amounts to sheer gimmickry.

Mr Howl went on to say that he would not hesitate to:

SLAP DOWN any sub who wrote dreary and involved head-lines,

ABUSE any sub who presented him with dull, tortuous intros that ran to about 15 lines of 12 point, and

THUMP any sub who failed to give him a bottle of Scotch on the third Thursday in every month.

Words in black caps

These were the changes announc-ed by Mr Bridlington:

1 All subs would in future be paid a minimum of £100 a week, and no reporter more than £30.

2 Subs would work three four-hour shifts a week, and report-ers six eight-hour shifts.

3 Cars would be withdrawn from reporters and specialists and given to subs.

Drop figures

Mr Howl went on to say that he would not hesitate to

● SLAP DOWN any sub who wrote dreary and involved head-lines,

● ABUSE any sub who presented him with dull, tortuous intros that ran to about 15 lines of 12 point, and

● THUMP any sub who failed to give him a bottle of Scotch on the third Thursday in every month.

Black blobs

These were the changes announc-ed by Mr Bridlington:

Pay: All subs would in future be paid a minimum of £100 a week, and no reporter more than £30.

Hours: Subs would work three four-hour shifts a week, and reporters six eight-hour shifts.

Perks: Cars would be with-drawn from reporters and special-ists and given to subs.

Contrasting type

These were the changes announc-ed by Mr Bridlington:

① All subs would in future be paid a minimum of £100 a week, and no reporter more than £30.

② Subs would work three four-hour shifts a week, and reporters six eight-hour shifts.

③ Cars would be withdrawn from reporters and specialists and given to subs.

White on black figures

Mr Stimpson added that he had seen Jackson approach Miss Robertson in the office and lay his hand on her arm. She had not appeared to object.

The next witness was Mr Revor Tross, who said he was an early home copy-taster. There was laughter when the judge remark-ed: "You should be on What's My Line."

Mr Tross said that he had noticed that Jackson and Miss Robertson appeared to be on friendly terms, but had never sus-pected that Jackson's intentions were serious.

Vertical rule

There are many other permutations but these are enough for the average sub's armoury.

Headline types and styles

It is a virtue in a sub to be able to recognise instantly the face and the size of any type in regular newspaper use. That is not terribly difficult when it's realised just how few there are.

Probably the most widely-used of all type families in British newspapers today is Century, and there is good reason for it. It has a splendid vigour and bluntness which makes it ideal for the purpose. Its very lack of refinement and dignity, as compared say with Bodoni, actually helps in this respect. Its variety and versatility could not be demonstrated better than by the fact that it provides the basic display type for so many newspapers.

These are examples from the range that, except possibly for an occasional sans "kicker", can make other types unnecessary:

Century Bold

THE PRESS IS DOING A GREAT AND G
The Press is doing a great and good job

Century Bold Italic

THE PRESS IS DOING A GREAT JOB
The Press is doing a great and good job

Century Schoolbook

THE PRESS IS DOING A GREAT JO
The Press is doing a great and good jo

Century Schoolbook Bold

THE PRESS IS DOING A GREAT J
The Press is doing a great and good

Century Bold Extended

THE PRESS IS DOING A GRE
The Press is doing a great and g

Century Bold Condensed

THE PRESS IS DOING A GREAT JOB
The Press is doing a great and good job

The main sans face in use is the splendid Ludlow Medium Condensed Gothic, the main display face for *The Mirror* and the "kicker" face for many seriffed papers. Here it is in all its glory:

Medium Condensed Gothic

THE PRESS IS DOING A GREAT AND GO
The Press is doing a great and good j

What of the rest — the ancient but still-battling Cheltenham,* the over-perfect Bodoni, the useful Caslon with its unhappy italic, the neglected Plantin, the Times Bold with its successful but under-used lower case, the thundering Placard so splendidly used by the *Daily Sketch*, the varied square Grotesques, and the Ludlow Tempo family?

All are capable of being used to produce sound newspapers. All *are* being used to produce sound newspapers. Here they are, with my comments on their virtues and failings:

Cheltenham Bold

THE PRESS IS DOING A GREAT JO
The Press is doing a great and good job

---

*Of which Allen Hutt (and here I'm speaking from memory) once remarked that although ancient compositors said "You can't beat Chelt" you can, only too easily.

147

Cheltenham Bold italic

THE PRESS IS DOING A GREAT JO
The Press is doing a great and good job

Old-fashioned, lacking the sharpness of Century, but still capable of being the basis for a handsome newspaper. It also has one virtue not demonstrated here — an enormous number of variants. They include a Bold Condensed, a Bold Extra Condensed, a Bold Expanded.

Bodoni Bold

THE PRESS IS DOING A GREAT AND G
The Press is doing a great and good job

Bodoni Bold italic

THE PRESS IS DOING A GREAT AND
The Press is doing a great and good job

Elegant, sharp, a thing of beauty — indeed, perhaps too beautiful to be entirely satisfactory for a newspaper which wants to give an impression of vigour and bluntness. Its italic is especially good — but note that there are different versions available which vary a great deal in colour. Bodoni Bold is very small on the body compared with most faces used by newspapers: compare the lines above with their same-size Century equivalents. Other members of the family include Bodoni (a much lighter face), Bodoni Bold Condensed, and the swashbuckling Ultra Bodoni, which properly used can add something to any newspaper, but wrongly used will make it look like a Victorian steam laundry handbill.

Caslon Heavy

THE PRESS IS DOING A GREAT J
The Press is doing a great and good job

Caslon Heavy italic

THE PRESS IS DOING A GREAT JO
The Press is doing a great and good job

Caslon Bold Condensed

THE PRESS IS DOING A GREAT JOB
The Press is doing a great and good job

A strong face in the roman, though somehow lacking the urgency of Century Bold. Its italic is far from successful, and the bigger it is the unhappier it looks; the old London *Star* used it in all its enormity, never with any great joy.

Plantin Bold

THE PRESS IS DOING A GREAT
The Press is doing a great and good jo

Plantin Bold italic

THE PRESS IS DOING A GREAT
The Press is doing a great and good

A blunt, rather thumping face. The basic Plantin, a lighter face, is a suitable variant, but on its own is too fine for newspaper work.

Times Bold

THE PRESS IS DOING A GREAT JO
The Press is doing a great and good job

Times Heavy Titling

THE PRESS IS DOING A GREAT AND G

Times Extended Titling

THE PRESS IS DOING A GREA

A magnificent family, full of contrast and colour. This particularly applies to the vigorous lower case of the bold, which is big on its body and more condensed than the caps would lead to expect. (Indeed the width of the Bold Titling seems nearer to it.)

Placard Bold Condensed

THE PRESS IS DOING A GREAT JOB
The Press is doing a great and good job

Placard Condensed

THE PRESS AND COWDREY ARE DOING A GREAT JOB
The Press and Cowdrey are doing a great job

A touch of the bludgeon in Placard Bold, but a vigorous, readable type. Both the Bold and the Bold Condensed are exceptionally big on the body.

Grotesque Bold

THE PRESS IS DOING A GREAT J
The Press is doing a great and goo

Grotesque Bold

THE PRESS IS DOING A GREA
The Press is doing a great and

Square Gothic

THE PRESS IS DOING A GREAT J
The Press is doing a great and good

Record Gothic Bold Medium Extended

THE PRESS IS DOING A GREAT JOB
The Press is doing a great job

The Grots and Square Gothics are used by a number of papers, but tend to give a rather slow and over-leisurely feeling. The *Sunday Express* used them for years but dropped them in favour of the Century family.

Tempo Bold

THE PRESS AND COWDREY ARE DOING
The Press and Cowdrey are doing a great

Tempo Bold Condensed

THE PRESS AND COWDREY ARE DOING A GREAT
The Press and Cowdrey are doing a great job

Tempo Heavy

THE PRESS AND COWDREY ARE DOIN
The Press and Cowdrey are doing a gree

Tempo Heavy Italic

THE PRESS AND COWDREY ARE DOIN
The Press and Cowdrey are doing a gre

Tempo Heavy Condensed Italic

THE PRESS AND COWDREY ARE DOING A GREAT AN
The Press and Cowdrey are doing a great and good jol

A case of splendid, vigorous italics with a parent roman which in my view has a poster-ish quality which makes it an unhappy choice for newspapers. The Heavy Condensed Italic is outstandingly good and sorts well with the Ludlow Medium Condensed Gothic.

There are a number of other sans faces in the Linotype and Intertype ranges, including the well-tried Metro and Vogue, but these, of course, are only available in the smaller sizes.

One other modern family deserves mention, and that is the elegant Univers. As far as I know no major newspaper has yet based itself entirely on Univers, but with the vast range now available there seems no good reason why not. A quality newspaper keeping firmly inside that one family is perfectly feasible. The present range includes Bold, Bold Condensed, Bold Expanded, Extra Bold, Extra Bold Expanded, Light, Light Condensed, Medium, Medium Condensed, Medium Expanded and Ultra Bold Extended, and that should be enough for anybody. Here are a few of them:

Univers Bold

THE PRESS IS DOING A GREAT AND GO
The Press is doing a great and good job

Univers Bold Expanded

THE PRESS IS DOING A GREAT JO
The Press is doing a great and good

Univers Light

THE PRESS IS DOING A GREAT AND GOOD J
The Press is doing a great and good job

Univers Medium

THE PRESS IS DOING A GREAT AND GOOD
The Press is doing a great and good job

Univers Ultra Bold Expanded

THE PRESS IS DOING A GREAT J
The Press is doing a great and go

The question of styles of headline is much simpler than it used to be. In the beginning was the multi-decker, enriched with full points, which was not so much a headline as a summary of what followed in the solid text below. It was inevitably all in caps and divided into its various parts by a mixture of plain or diamond rules. It drew attention to the surprising nature of the intelligence that followed. Translated into present-day terms, if there had been an election in which the Tories were returned with a majority of 200 in direct contradiction of the opinion polls, the Prime Minister had committed hari-kari in a northern fish and chip shop immediately the trend was known and the Leader of the Opposition had announced that he was secretly married to a well-known actress, the form would have been something like this:

THE GENERAL ELECTION.

SURPRISING RESULT.

CONSERVATIVES IN THE MAJORITY.

400 COMMONS SEATS.

PREMIER'S SAD END.

A SECRET MARRIAGE.

TORY LEADER AND ACTRESS.

In these days, of course, the headline would get right to the point.

BEATEN PREMIER SHOOTS HIMSELF

and have a nice human "separate" saying

My husband and I— by Fenella of No. 10

We are now moving more and more into the era of the single-deck headline, at any rate on the popular newspapers: the one thought that can be absorbed instantly.

This is often modified, of course. The splash and the big page lead will often have a couple of decks, sometimes with the motive of typographical variety. Occasionally a single-column top will appear likewise, but this now usually happens when the story is better told with two points in happy juxtaposition.

Another modern characteristic is the heavy preponderance of lower-case headings, a complete reversal of the early days of newspapers when an all-cap style was employed. Realisation of the greater legibility of lower case has led some newspapers to abandon cap headings altogether.

Taking the single-deck heading as the norm, there are certain points which need to be watched.

THE FIT. The best headline is no good if it busts. It is one thing to persuade the chief sub to change the type, but quite another to send it to the Printer in a desperate hope that it can be squeezed in. Far better to undercount and get a headline with a bit of air each side.

It is useful to bear in mind the differing width of letters. A rough and ready guide with lower case is to take these letters as one unit.

a b c d e g h k n o p q r s u v y z

to count

w m

as one and a half units, and

f i j l t

as half units. In some faces the letter "x" is one unit plus.

With caps, only the "I" can be counted as half a unit, with the "J" sometimes under the single unit. The "W" and "M" are usually not more than one and a half units.

Note that the figures of most faces are not the same width as the caps, although they are the same height. Thus although the word

CASH

may bust, the actual sum

£200

will get in, although it's the same number of units.

THE SHAPE. British newspapers use the main style for headings — centred and set (or range, or squared) left:

<table>
<tr><td>

Film star
dies in
night club

</td><td>

Film star
dies in
night club

</td></tr>
</table>

Less common forms are the set right, which always looks eccentric and hard to read to me, and the staggered:

Film star
dies in
night club

Film star
killed in
night club

Points to note on **centred** headings: avoid having all lines of equal length, which is monotonous; try to get a sequence of long-short-long-short to help the eye along; and allow at least a nut clearance between the widest line and the column rules to avoid a cramped appearance.

Ranged left. Here the sequence can be long-short-long-short or short-long-short-long, both giving a balanced appearance. Keeping away from the column rule is here even more important, and the heading should either be indented a pica left, or set with the longest line centred and the others ranged left on it. (Printers can be trained to understand the simple instruction "Range left and centre".)

Ranged right: Long-short-long-short is essential. Reverse it and the heading seems to fade away at the top. Indention rules apply as for ranged left, only back to front.

Staggered: Here it is essential to have all lines near-equal, or the result will look like a setting error. All these lines must, of course, be under full measure — say a couple of ems in a single column heading set nut each side.

PUNCTUATION. This should be ignored for centring or ranging headings. The effect of taking it into account is to upset the optical balance. Note how the first heading of this pair appears to be thrown out of tune.

Britt
‘is a big
success’

Britt
‘is a big
success’

The same applies in a centred headline, and the fault seen here becomes more marked as the size of the heading grows:

Howell
strikes –
and subs
revolt

Howell
strikes –
and subs
revolt

Warning note: Never regard the improved appearance as a justification for using a load of punctuation in a heading. Gimmicks apart, the less punctuation the better.

Subheads, plain and fancy

The subhead falls into two main styles:

1. THE CROSSHEAD, which is centred on the text. Care should be taken that crossheads are less than text-width, or the story will be sliced into sections; and also that they are all of similar width to avoid an uneven appearance.

2. THE SIDEHEAD, called in some offices a shoulder-head, is ranged left on the text. With hot metal the vital words are *on the text.* A story set pica each side should have sideheads indented pica left, otherwise an ugly overhang will result. But note that it is no use marking a 14 point sidehead em left and expecting it to match up with a story set 8 point, em each side. The em indent in the text will be an "em of the body", that is 8 points.

Whichever style is used it is important to bear in mind that the function of the ordinary common-or-garden subhead is primarily an optical one. Indications are that they are not consciously absorbed, but serve to rest the reader's eye as he ploughs through slabs of text. The specially-displayed crossheads, which are dealt with later, are in a different category.

It is not possible to give any real guidance on the frequency with which subheads should be used, because this again is largely a visual thing. The most that can be said is that narrow columns need more than wide columns, and that large subheads can be less frequent than small ones.

Types of crossheads and sideheads can be divided into two main groups.

1. BLACK OF TEXT. This is the oldest and among local papers still the most common form of breaker. It is adhered to not because it is a thing of beauty or even optically particularly effective, but simply because it is the most compatible with the resources available. When this applies it is necessary to use only the bold CAPS of the body face and watch the spacing with care. These examples show bold c + lc unspaced and bold caps correctly spaced:

He said that Mr Sewell would undoubtedly make a most distinguished member of Parliament and be a credit to the Woodside division of Glasgow.

He said that Mr Sewell would undoubtedly make a most distinguished member of Parliament and be a credit to the Woodside division of Glasgow.

No Trouble
It did not seem likely that he would have any trouble with the Scottish Nationalists, who were likely to change their allegiance when they discovered his virtues.

NO TROUBLE
It did not seem likely that he would have any trouble with the Scottish Nationalists, who were likely to change their allegiance when they discovered his virtues.

2. LARGER THAN TEXT. These provide a far more satisfactory breaker in the body matter, and a large number of suitable faces are available. It is essential to choose those which can be set with speed and simplicity. It is also desirable to choose a fount which can be fully utilised elsewhere, and for practical purposes this means one used for the bigger intros. The ideal size for an 11¼ em column is 12 or 14 point, according to the weight and width of the face chosen, with correspondingly larger sizes for subheads in broad measure setting.

Larger-than-text subheads come in two main styles:

Matching the display. A paper based on Century Bold might have subheads of Century Bold, Century Schoolbook or Century Extended, either in caps or lower case. Whatever is chosen should be clearly distinguishable from headings on shorts: a paper using Century Bold c + lc centred for shorts should not use the same for crossheads.

These examples of single-line crossheads are all from the Century range:

He said that Mr Sewell would undoubtedly make a most distinguished member of Parliament and be a credit to the Woodside division of Glasgow.

No trouble

It did not seem likely that he would have any trouble with the Scottish Nationalists, who were likely to change their allegiance when they discovered his virtues.

He said that Mr Sewell would undoubtedly make a most distinguished member of Parliament and be a credit to the Woodside division of Glasgow.

No trouble

It did not seem likely that he would have any trouble with the Scottish Nationalists, who were likely to change their allegiance when they discovered his virtues.

He said that Mr Sewell would undoubtedly make a most distinguished member of Parliament and be a credit to the Woodside division of Glasgow.

NO TROUBLE

It did not seem likely that he would have any trouble with the Scottish Nationalists, who were likely to change their allegiance when they discovered his virtues.

He said that Mr Sewell would undoubtedly make a most distinguished member of Parliament and be a credit to the Woodside division of Glasgow.

No trouble

It did not seem likely that he would have any trouble with the Scottish Nationalists, who were likely to change their allegiance when they discovered his virtues.

Contrasting face. Here the "intro" faces such as Helvetica, Vogue, Galaxy and Metro are all satisfactory, but need carefully watching for weight. Metromedium, for example, needs to be a size larger than Vogue Extra Bold to get a similar effect. These four examples are in Helvetica Bold, Vogue Bold, Metroblack and Galaxy Bold:

He said that Mr Sewell would undoubtedly make a most distinguished member of Parliament and be a credit to the Woodside division of Glasgow.

No trouble

It did not seem likely that he would have any trouble with the Scottish Nationalists, who were likely to change their allegiance when they discovered his virtues.

He said that Mr Sewell would undoubtedly make a most distinguished member of Parliament and be a credit to the Woodside division of Glasgow.

No trouble

It did not seem likely that he would have any trouble with the Scottish Nationalists, who were likely to change their allegiance when they discovered his virtues.

He said that Mr Sewell would undoubtedly make a most distinguished member of Parliament and be a credit to the Woodside division of Glasgow.

NO TROUBLE

It did not seem likely that he would have any trouble with the Scottish Nationalists, who were likely to change their allegiance when they discovered his virtues.

He said that Mr Sewell would undoubtedly make a most distinguished member of Parliament and be a credit to the Woodside division of Glasgow.

NO TROUBLE

It did not seem likely that he would have any trouble with the Scottish Nationalists, who were likely to change their allegiance when they discovered his virtues.

Spacing of subheads, as indicated above, needs the greatest care if they are to serve their full optical function. The reason is simple: Subheads provide the stonehand with the easiest way out if a story drops too long or too short.

A desirable spacing rule in hot metal would be:

BLACK OF TEXT: Five points above and three points below.

LARGER THAN TEXT: Seven points above and four below.

With photosetting, the eyes have it. The variation above and below has the effect of relating the subhead more closely to the section it covers.

A rule such as this forces the stonehand to ask for cuts if the story is overlong; or forces him either to find a filler or space the story the hard way if it falls short.

One final, unbreakable rule on simple subheads: they should never be allowed to turn into a second line.

Now to the fancier, big-time crossheads and sideheads. These are either reserved for the major story, or (and this is infinitely preferable) planned with as much care as the heading to fit a particular story.

The intention may be to establish a theme, provide major breaks in a story occupying the greater part of a page, or perhaps to introduce a special effect into a long single-column story. This kind of subhead can be grouped into four main varieties:

1. UNDERSCORED. The scoring of subheads should not be over-done, or the usefulness of the device will be lost. Care should be taken that the thickness of the score bears some relation to the weight of the type above it. If it's too light it will pass almost unnoticed; if too heavy it will kill the subhead. A subhead in Schoolbook would marry happily with a fine score, but Schoolbook Bold calls for a 2 point, and a great thumping type like Ultra Bodoni or Ludlow Black will take a 3 point.

Beware of using decorative rules as underscores. Apart from overpowering the words they have such an ultra-featurish effect they need using with extreme care even on features.

2. MULTI-LINE. These need a long story to justify their existence, for they are both space-consuming and an obstruction put in the way of the clean flow of the story. Yet they should not be ignored, for they are a splendid device for dividing the "long read" into sub-compartments.

It is particularly important that they should not be capable of confusion with headings on shorts. This does not necessarily exclude the use of the same type: if headings on shorts are centred, 2-line subheadings can be ranged left, and vice-versa.

With two-line subheads a consistent shape is needed to give a visual identity — long-short for crossheads and short-long for sideheads.

A useful variant, especially in establishing a theme in a story, is the subhead which consists of one line of caps and one of lower case. It is effective in three permutations: roman caps and roman lower case, roman caps and italic lower case, and italic caps and italic lower case. Combining italic caps and roman lower case produces an unhappy distortion, as can be seen in these examples:

FOOT	**MAGGIE**
gets voted out	*gets voted in*
STEELE	*JENKINS*
gets voted tops	**gets voted off**

Use the first three styles, but avoid the last.

3. BOXED. Here there are three things to watch:

Ensure that the box is narrower than the text — a pica or so is needed or the read-through will be affected.

Ensure that the rule is not so heavy that it kills the type within and jumps obtrusively out of the page. A fine rule is normally adequate, but the small dot border is attractive, too.

Break the rules top and bottom to lessen the dividing effect of the box. These two examples show the good and the bad in box crossheads:

He said that Mr Sewell would undoubtedly make a most distinguished member of Parliament and be a credit to the Woodside division of Glasgow.

No trouble

It did not seem likely that he would have any trouble with the Scottish Nationalists, who were likely to change their allegiance when they discovered his virtues.

He said that Mr Sewell would undoubtedly make a most distinguished member of Parliament and be a credit to the Woodside division of Glasgow.

No trouble

It did not seem likely that he would have any trouble with the Scottish Nationalists, who were likely to change their allegiance when they discovered his virtues.

4. DECORATIVE. These are of use only in feature pages or diaries, and then are to be used with caution. A common form is to precede the subhead with a matching star, black for heavier faces and open for light faces; or with a matching blob for the heavier faces.

Two more complex variants, using vertical stars and a vertical rule, which have cropped up from time to time:

One thing's for sure: your friend and mine will be invited to attend.

 **FASHION**

GLAMOROUS Jeanne Handforth, blonde ex-model fiancee of one of our brighter MPs, will be in London next week to compere a series of fashion shows.

One thing's for sure: your friend and mine will be invited to attend.

 Fashion

GLAMOROUS Jeanne Handforth, blonde ex-model fiancee of one of our brighter MPs, will be in London next week to compere a series of fashion shows.

The basis of design

This is not the place for a detailed discussion on newspaper design, but on the principle that all subs ought to have some knowledge of the rudiments it is worth while setting down a few of the main points. Here are four good rules:

1. **KEEP IT FLEXIBLE**
2. **KEEP IT SIMPLE**
3. **AIM FOR CONTRAST**
4. **WATCH YOUR BOTTOM. IT NEEDS AS MANY KICKS AS IT CAN GET.**

A quick rundown on each point:

1. FLEXIBILITY is the very essence of good newspaper design, because of the overriding need to let the news come first. The most attractive page ever drawn must be thrown aside without a second thought if something which is better from a content point of view comes along. The special projection that has been toiled over long and hard must be cut down to size if a new development demands.

No one concerned with designing a newspaper page must ever fall in love with its beauty. The design exists only as a means to sell the news, and if the news changes the page must change too.

2. SIMPLICITY rates highly. The design must make the page *easier* to read, not harder. The ordinary customer takes things from left to right and from top to bottom: that's the way his Learn to Read books were laid out.

This is a fundamental point to bear in mind whenever a page is in danger of becoming like a game of snakes and ladders in which they eye is constantly being switched from place to place, or a jumble of types which only bedazzle and bemuse.

3. CONTRAST should be sought, and it is important here to bear in mind the advertisements in the page. Points to note here are:

If the ads are symmetrical — say two 3 × 11s in a broadsheet page — then the design should veer to the asymmetrical. But faced with a 5 × 13 or 5 × 15 solus the editorial trend should be towards a symmetrical design to restore the balance of the page.

If the ads are introducing a lot of tone into the page then the editorial content should incline to the textual, and vice-versa.

If the ads are messy and bitty — say 5 × 13 store ads — then the adjacent editorial text should be plain. It's the only way to achieve the contrast which will give the editorial matter a chance.

The placing of the tone in ads should be always considered. If the bottom half of columns 4 to 8 in a broadsheet page consists of a half-tone block, then the editorial half-tone should incline to the top left-hand side to restore the balance.

In the cause of good contrast beware of long grey patches, and seek ways of breaking them up. Try to avoid having any column rule running from the top to the bottom of a page by properly utilising "stoppers".

A good rule here is never to place a double-column story directly under another double-column story, unless of course it's a straight tie-on or part of a sequence. Certainly avoid running one single-column top under another. Down-page tops should always appear in a natural angle.

And lastly

4. BOTTOMS are important. Many a good page has been ruined by a lack of attention to the stories below the fold. The bottom of a page needs just as much attention as the top. The three most important factors here are

Horizontal stresses. A broadsheet page needs at least one and usually more multi-column headlines to hold up the bottom.

Shorts. The presence of a good number of shorts, placed in runs in alternate columns give a busy appearance below the fold.

Half-tone. By the nature of advertising half-tones need using with care, but in multi-column gutters are sometimes needed.

The thoughts expounded above are necessarily very broad in character.

Basically the things needed by anyone designing a newspaper page are these:

1. A good news sense
2. A basic knowledge of typography
3. A strong visual sense
4. Practice, practice, practice.

Any sub feeling himself drawn to page design needs as much of No. 4 as possible. There are many opportunities of getting it, even unofficially. Redraw your own newspaper's pages when the chief sub's not looking. Grab the chance of doing slip pages where you have a chance to experiment.

The more you do, the easier and quicker it becomes. And the better the pages, if the aptitude is there.

12 COLOUR

Use any you like
and that includes black

COLOUR? What colour? The only colour this newspaper's got is black, and that's the only colour it's ever likely to have . . .

It's a sorrowful refrain, but too often true. Throughout the world major newspapers have been frightened by run-of-print colour, or more often by the trade unions and the prospect of a substantial capital investment going to waste.

But when you've got it, it can be wonderful.

One irony is that it's the smaller newspapers and the smaller countries that have taken to colour.

Look at the house newspapers and trade journals, printed on contract on machines such as the Goss Urbanite. Often using moderately-cheap paper, insofar as such a thing exists now, they manage a high standard of colour reproduction.

Similarly, some of the newspapers in the Mediterranean countries don't even need the drop of a hat to plaster their pages with colour. I'm sure if the great Allen Hutt had still been alive he would have used his copyright phrase "an obscene porridge" to describe the results in some cases.

And it's not all black and white in South Africa either: editorial use of run-of-print colour there is among the best as well as the most lavish in the world. The *Sunday Times,* based in Johannesburg but printing simultaneously in four centres up to 1000 miles apart, will frequently use 50 full colour pictures in one issue.

In Australia, where the major newspaper chains are still black and white, one independent proprietor told me that if they used a full colour picture on the front page they added one-fifth to the print order. And it's not without significance that Robert Holmes a Court is using colour lavishly in his bid to break into the Australian market.

All this leads me to the point that it's a good thing for every sub-editor to know something about putting colour in newspapers. You never know: some day those Page Three nipples might be the colour nature made them.

Two kinds of colour

I don't think the sub-editor or the editorial production genius needs to know the detailed mechanics of producing good rotary offset colour, any more than he needs to be a good photographer himself to know that he's got a good picture in his hands.

But he does need to know a few basic facts, so that he neither drops foolish clangers nor allows himself to be fooled into thinking that something can't be done when it can.

FACT ONE: There are three ink basic colours from which all others in full colour printing derive:

Cyan, which is British Airways blue;

Magenta, which is an off-red, vaguely more bluey than the traditional pillar-box red;

Yellow, which (surprise, surprise! Could anything be so simple?) is yellow.

To these you add *black,* and if you mix any two or three or even four of them in different proportions you can achieve any colour in the rainbow and many more besides.

Basically it's like a child's painting box. One of the first things you learn is that if you mix yellow and blue together you get green. Add a bit more blue or a bit more yellow and you get different shades of green.

To print a full colour picture you first have to get it back to the stage of separate primary colours, red, green and blue. Remember what happens when white light passing through a prism is separated into its component light rays to form a rainbow of colours. A highly sophisticated machine takes new pictures of the original. But by a series of filters it breaks down the fine shades of colour into their constituent parts — so much red, so much green, so much blue — and prints all the blue on one negative, all the green on a second negative and so on.

The end products are the *separations,* each containing only one of the primary colours. They are converted to the printing plates, which apply the printing inks to paper as filters. The red plate prints cyan ink which absorbs the red light rays falling on the paper, leaving the green and blue rays which, hallelujah, add up to cyan.

FACT TWO: It's important to differentiate between *full colour,* which prints the pictures (see above) and *spot colour,* which prints "spots" of colour — rules, borders, washes, tints, headings in a single colour.

The spot colour need not necessarily be one of the basic colours — cyan, magenta, or yellow.

IF it's being printed on a machine that's printing *only* spot colour it can use any colour of ink that's available from the manufacturer.

IF it's being printed as part of a full-colour operation it can be a basic colour or any percentage mixture of the basic colours. *But* at this point the accuracy of the spot colour may deteriorate — a purple cast or a brown, or an excessive amount of blue in what was intended to be grass green. The reason is that while the spot-only process may be using a pre-mixed purple or green, the other will be concentrating on getting the full colour right. So the spot colour may suffer.

What sort of pictures?

Oddly enough, many people (including me) find it easier and quicker to choose the right trannie than to do the same thing with black-and-white negs or contact prints.

The reason is that you can, given, say, 36 trannies on one subject, usually eliminate 20 of them *for reasons that don't apply with black-and-white*. So instead of having 36 frames to study you only have 16.

What gives?

OUT first go all pale or "desaturated" trannies. There's little that can be done to correct this fault — and if there *is* anything it's 99.9 per cent certain that in the pressures of newspaper production it won't be.

OUT go all trannies with a heavy "cast" of one colour or another. The most common "cast" is cyan, but that depends on light conditions in the area, and if it happens regularly a change to a different brand of film will probably help. Remember: You can modify a cyan "cast" at the separations stage by the use of filters, but it's better to avoid it if possible.

OUT goes confusing colour. If the columns are such that the subject doesn't leap out at you — avoid it. The photographer who shoots a woman in a green-and-yellow frock against a background of green-and-yellow shouldn't be allowed out anyway. But there are more modest muddles — the green of one subject running into the blue of another; overlapping broken surfaces where the merging effect is exaggerated by the colour; and overlapping figures in matching clothes.

After that, look at the rest for strong, clearly-defined colours that will leap out of the page and catch the eye.

After that, you're looking for the same qualities that you would do in black and white — detail, highlights, and — terribly important from a newspaper point of view — composition. A large area of unfunctional colour in the picture as printed is even more confusing than the same in black and white.

The mechanics of choosing

By long hallowed tradition, newspaper photographers have held up a strip of negs to the light, said "Those two will do" and carried on printing. With colour a bit more equipment is needed. At rock bottom you need —

A LIGHT BOX of some kind. This can be large or freestanding, or small and resting on a table. It can be ridged to take mounted slides, but this is far from essential. It will preferably have special fluorescent tubes as a light source

A LENS to study detail or to make a final difficult choice, or to confirm you haven't made the wrong one. A last check is generally wise — you might find when you see the blow-up that a freak of light has given the mayor a most disgusting runny nose, or that what you thought was ordinary shadow on a pin-up was actually the five o'clock variety.

Some offices use the kind of projector that throws an enlarged image on an inset panel. The models I've tried are excellent when in prime condition, but tend to pick up every bit of muck in the neighbourhood in every nook and cranny, with the result that they lose efficiency unless someone is deployed to clean them regularly.

The best way I know to "package" the trannies for viewing (and later filing) is to have them cut into strips and placed in a transparent folder. It almost goes without saying, I hope, that this must be identified with the usual Subject-Date-Photographer's Name info.

The prelim inspection can be done through the folder, thereby reducing the danger of greasy fingerprints, which the buggeration factor will almost certainly land on the trannie you'd have chosen if you hadn't made such a mess of it.

How to do a good cropping job

The cropping of full colour in newspapers is pretty abysmal. This is probably not surprising in the light of the conditions under which most newspapers work. But there is no excuse for some of the atrocities that get through: I almost cried when I saw in a broadsheet newspaper a front page picture *that had nothing but bright blue sky above the fold.*

The most usual method is to use a bit of Sellotape to attache the trannie to a sheet of copy paper and put marks on it to indicate where you want it cropped.

This is a vague and inadequate system, an acceptance of good luck taking over from good management, and an invitation to disaster. It doesn't allow for the smallness of the scale, nor the fact that the trannie has to be separated from its sheet of paper.

The best way I know out of this problem is to get the photographer to make a quick black and white print, quality irrelevant, or even a neg print if you're really pushed for time.

Once you've got that print you can get the measurements perfect. You can crop in tightly or choose which bit of atmosphere you want kept in. You can crop on the tilt, or cut round heads or feet, or plan heart-shaped pierces. In short, *you can do everything mentioned in Chapter 10.*

There is another point. The people who make the separations won't have the slightest excuse for screwing things up. They will get the blame for anything that goes wrong, and the editorial halo will remain untarnished.

So much for perfection. But suppose that however hard you try you can't get such a system working — and I believe that everyone concerned should try very hard.

There's a getout, although it's by no means as good as the original. On the market is a small desk-top gadget which in about one minute will give you a Polaroid print from any trannie. You can do some pretty accurate cropping on these.

Much to be said for it, and not much against

THIS chapter has a demerit that is alien to newspaper thinking and caused me to pause many times before attempting it: it's vague. But I could see no way of avoiding either the chapter or the vagueness — the first because electronic editing is busting out all over, and the second because the amount subs are allowed to do within the system ranges from everything to nothing.

I don't intend to become involved in a union war. Yet after ten years' involvement in electronic systems, I feel bound to say that I find the resistance understandable but in the end humiliating to those concerned. Setting Stock Exchange prices on an obsolete and dirty piece of machinery is the equivalent of making gas mantles. My experience is that after the initial hiccup modern methods of newspaper production create jobs because they make it a game a lot more people can play. Starting from scratch, London could have ten evening newspapers instead of one.

That is not to say all is sweetness and light. If a newspaper goes the whole way into electronics the sub's job changes — and more subs are needed. This is because the sub is effectively typesetting the copy *and* doing the reader's job as well. If he gets one letter or digit wrong in the setting instructions he could end up with the entire story set in 72 pt instead of 7 pt, and a bromide 15 metres long instead of a few centimetres. If he types in *relavent* or *relevant* (which is my personal bit of subbing dyslexia) that's the way it will appear in the page. The sub is the long stop as well as the opening bat.

In practice, of course, there will be certain checks in most newspapers — *but they will be editorial ones.*

What does "going the whole way" involve? In effect it means emulating the Russian peasant who leapt on the English lady travelling on the Trans-Siberian express, grunting "No time for the preliminary stages — off with your drawers!"

IT MEANS skipping the period of subbing-by-ballpoint on hard copy prepared on a steam typewriter, and then having it retyped by a retreaded lino-op. It certainly means a firm No to the absurdity of subbing on a video screen, printing it out on an electronic printer, and then having it re-input, complete with mistakes for readers to correct.

IT MEANS reporters inputting directly on to the screen and into the computer (most of them learn to love video screens and hate typewriters within 48 hours), and queue-switching their copy to the subs, who after doing their best or worst will convert it to cold type.

The duties that now befall the sub include all those that have gone before, plus additional ones to slow him down and in some cases dull his wits.

Some problems fall away. He no longer needs to guess how long the story is, or employ one of those complicated systems of casting off beloved of some training schools. He presses the button marked HJ (for hyphenate and justify) and within seconds he has the length to one-tenth of a centimetre.

A busting — or shy — heading is a thing of the past. The computer will instantly report back how many characters it is over or under. The computer will also provide, if the editor sees fit to trust his subs so far, a "make it fit" facility. If the headline doesn't fit in 72 pt × 83.6 ems, you have freedom, dear electronic brain, to size it down to 68.3 pt, or up to 74.6 pt, and who will know the difference? The old joke about rubber type, that for generations has given comps a feeling of superiority over subs, has become reality.

And in more ways than giving you sizes of type from, say, 5 pt to 96 pt, *in graduations of one-tenth of a point*. The computer can also reduce the spacing between characters so that a heading that might bust by one character will miraculously fit. If that fails it can change the set width of the type to provide letters that are, for example, the full depth of a 30 pt character but the width of a 27 pt one.

This is clearly a recipe for chaos. Unlimited freedom to change the depth, width, and spacing of letters would produce an unrecognisable newspaper that would change from day to day. Century Bold would get so mucked around that in some cases it would look like Century Condensed and in others like a grubby version of Century Extended. Page leads would have 47 pt or 86 pt headings instead of 72 pt and the page would lose its balance.

In some cases power is given to the computer to adjust size, spacing and set width up to a fixed maximum — perhaps four per cent either way, which is unrecognisable to the ordinary reader.

Other newspapers give the sub a bit of leeway, and the chief sub-editor a bit more. But it must be restricted to preserve the identity of the paper.

Here are some advantages that the sub should utilise:

1. *PERFECT FIT* — and a good shape, too, for the pattern of minuses against each line of heading on the screen will indicate how it will look. Remember, too, to take advantage of a bit of leeway in size.

2. *PERFECT FIT* in copy. Try to achieve by eliminating surplus words, and particularly those widow words at the end of paragraphs. Now you can see them on the screen.

3. *WELL-FITTING* multi-column captions. No longer should the odd word or two turn over into the next line.

4. *INTROS* of readable length. Now you know whether a single-column intro makes a reasonable five lines or an inedible ten, or whether a 3-column par makes three lines plus one lonely word.

And more than anything else . . .

FIND OUT how to do all the things that the system will let you do if you know how — set 6-line drop letters; inset blobs, squares, crossed knives and forks, stars of David and 36-pt Santa Clauses; reverse type, slope it, or put it in a box or a tint. That's what the new technology is about.

But it does raise the question that has occupied many involved in subbing in the new and inevitable technological age: Is the present organisation right?

Is it reasonable to expect that a man who can do the classic subbing job of taking information from a number of sources and turning it into a smooth, flowing, well-written story should necessarily be an able technician? Or that a man who can write a story that will make a reader laugh or cry, or a heading that will make him jump in his chair, must also know the magic formula that gives 8 on 8½ pt Crown bold × 9.6 ems, ragged right, cancel hyphenation?

Perhaps the answer is the system that was used by many American newspapers even in hot metal days, and have rewrite editors (who knocked up the jewelled prose) and copy editors, who attended to the technicalities.

That way, in a sense, we'd be back with comps again, which is a bit ironic. But somewhere in that direction may lie the future of subbing.

INDEX